Soul Ties

Soul Ties:

What are they?
How are they formed?
How can they be broken forever?

Elaine Rose Penn

Soul Ties

First Printing, 2000
ISBN: 0-9700449-0-9

Unless otherwise indicated,
all scripture quotations in this volume
are from the *King James Version* of the Bible

Published by Chrisma Training Ministries
P.O. Box 2410
Albany, New York 12220-0410
epenn3@juno.com (email address)

For more information,
or to order additional copies
of this book, please contact CTM
at the above address.

Cover illustration by Robert Crentsil

Backcover photo by Loreli Burkhouse, *The Country Studio*

Printed in the United States by:
Morris Publishing
3212 East Highway 30
Kearney, NE 68847
1-800-650-7888

This book is dedicated to
Visionary Venus Bush
and
the Women of Fort Wayne, Indiana

You didn't just believe that I
could do this, but you expected me to.

Acknowledgements

Because this is my first effort, there are so many that I am indebted to for its completion. Among the many who have lent their love and support, I wish to extend to the following my deepest gratitude:

To my dear supporters, **Sandy Leavitt and Sandra Downer,** for your financial support, your faith in my God-given abilities, and your prayers. **Sandy**, what a precious friend and prayer partner you are in my life. Your comments and questions during the manuscript phase of this book helped me to reach toward excellence.

To **Jacquié McIver**, my long time friend. I knew that you had greatness in you. Thank you for believing in me.

To **Apostle James R. Jones**, you were the first one who believed in me. I have tried ever since to live out the charge that you placed on my life. When I came under your pastoral guidance, you broke my chains, and helped me to fly. The counsel you gave me in those early days, still guides me.

To **Apostle Norman Rochford** who left this life in April 1999 to join our Lord. His teaching and insights regarding soul ties and the power of the marriage relationship spurred me on to deeper and deeper study of this topic. I shall see him again one day in Paradise, until then, I do so miss him.

To **Pastor Rose Stuart**, a visionary indeed. There are many women of God that I hold in high esteem... but none higher than you. Although it has cost you dearly, still, you dare to obey the Savior.

To my parents, **Lula M. Penn of Maryland**, and **Willis and Louise Penn of Florida**, not only did you give me life, but you gave me Jesus at a tender age. Thank you for loving and supporting me... and for being proud of me.

To **Apostle Benjamin Thomas**, my spiritual father who has gone home to be with our Lord. Will I ever become what you saw in me? You told me to always be true to God... I promise I will.

To **Rita Thomas**, you hold such a special place in my heart. I have every single card and treasure that you sent with our four-footed friend on it. Nobody, not even time, can destroy those memories.

To **Crystal Alexander**, my sister and one of my biggest fans. What a gift you are in my life.

To the **Ramsey Family**, thank you for many precious memories.

To the **Tuesday Prayer Group**, there are just no words to express what each and every one of you mean to me... **Betty, Sandy, Tanya, Frank, Jerry, Diane, Larry, Helga, Georgette, Karen, Sue and Lou**.

To my brother, best friend, and co-laborer in the gospel, **Apostle Robert Crentsil**... we're bonded for life. Your scriptural insights provided the final touches to this book. It is as much a product of who you are as I.

To **Henry Polk**, my trusted friend and brother. In the moments when I've grown weary of life, you've assured me that there was yet a reason to hope. In those moments, I trusted you and believed you and discovered that you were right.

To **Wallace Pete**, my friend, mentor, and counselor. You are a tremendous blessing in my life. Thank you for always being there when I need you.

To **Connie McDaniels and Romaine Frank**, my personal intercessors. I'd be a dead woman if the two of you didn't fight for me the way you do.

To my dearest **Cetra**, my daughter. You've given me more than I'll ever be able to repay in a lifetime. You've given me the greatest gift of all... you call me "Mom."

And, last but not least, to Jesus, my Lord and Savior, without you I can do nothing.

Foreword

I have taught in the areas of Kingdom authority and breaking generational curses for many years. I have also spent a great deal of time counseling and ministering to the people of God who were at various depths of bondage. Both in my teaching and administering deliverance, I kept experiencing a quiet dissatisfaction with the results. I'd see individuals free for a moment, and right back in the grips of bondage and demonic slavery the next. It was disconcerting to promise hope, but not see it become a reality in their lives. I kept wondering what I was doing wrong.

In my quest to become better at deliverance ministry, I kept searching for tools. My search led me to book upon book, tapes — video and audio, conference after conference... and while I became stronger and more knowledgeable... I still didn't see the kind of results experienced by the early church. I kept on wondering what I was doing wrong.

Then I turned to the victims themselves to determine if, in fact, their inability to be set free had to do with some insidious part of their humanness or spirituality that hindered my attempts to set them free. Clearly, there was nothing wrong with the Holy Spirit or his methods. I had checked and double-checked my own motives, my methods, and base of knowledge. What was wrong with the victims, that they couldn't get free? What was wrong with me, as a deliverance minister, that I couldn't put the axe to the root?

Then a major trauma hit my life and sent me reeling. The pains of death took a hold of me... I discovered, to my horror, what it felt like to have a broken spirit. I lost my way; my self-esteem was shattered. My soul descended into an indescribable darkness that I could feel. I limped — broken, bruised and bleeding to the arms of Jesus, hoping with quiet desperation, that what I had preached and taught for so many years would now work for me. I had never felt so alone and defenseless in all of my life. What if the enemy caught me like this, at this moment? I was as good as a dead woman... he and I were sworn enemies.

Then, I began to experience an unusual thing. Angels, who had once appeared to me when I was a young girl of 3 or 4, began to surround me and make their presence felt. At times, I could see their visage... brighter than the noon day sun. They would hover around me, reaching to touch me, reassure me, vigilantly taking their turns to hold me and strengthen me. These were times I would sit and weep at the feet of Jesus, distraught, with my life draining and ebbing away. They would sit with me — these angelic brothers of mine, encircling me, desperate to keep their charge over my life. But it was the Holy Spirit who accomplished the greater work.

Into my soul he went, cutting and scraping away the poison and dead things that occurred in the winter times of my life. There were times when I was afraid that he would cut too deeply, but I discovered that the hand of the Potter is sure. He took me back, in the soul realm, to early hurts, early disappointments, and deep wounds of rejection. Into my soul he went even further, cutting deeper and deeper, making small, strategic incisions... deep calling unto deep. The pain was at times gut-wrenching, as he exposed issue after issue. What I thought had been erased, had actually been carefully inventoried and catalogued by my soul. All of it was still there, festering, growing, rotting, and poisoning my entire destiny. My God... I had been preaching, teaching, testifying, and dancing over open graves in my own soul. I knew then that never again in my walk with the Lord, would I ever let gifts impress me.

While He was in there, he did an awesome work in my life. A process that I thought would surely kill me, raised me to a brand new level. A new woman emerged... the old woman died a slow, agonizing death. Which was greater? My actual deliverance, or what I had learned? I had watched the Holy Spirit very carefully as he operated on me... I wondered, if, with his help, I could become a better minister to others. I wondered if what he had done for me would work for any case... no matter how tough. I began to study the soul... this place of decaying flesh, graveclothes and sepulchers; this place that preachers never spoke about. A new, triumphant woman emerged from the abyss — a woman with a deeper understanding about bondage and what it takes to get free.

This work is a culmination of teaching and preaching on the issues of soul ties, forbidden covenants, and generational curses, and kingdom authority. I am forever grateful to the Body of Christ, far and near, for nudging me to greater and greater revelation on the topic. Every question and concern raised by seminar participants over the years has broadened my quest for deeper knowledge and revelation on the topic of soul ties. I pray that in reading this book, you will be changed forever... after the likeness of our soon coming King, Jesus.

Elaine Rose Penn, Author

Table of Contents

Chapter One

The Soul

"And the very God of peace sanctify you wholly; and I pray God your whole spirit and soul and body be preserved blameless unto the coming of our Lord Jesus Christ." 1 Thessalonians 5:23

What is the Soul?

We are triune beings, which means we are comprised of three essential parts: our spirit, soul, and body. And, although each part is distinctive from the other two (James 2:26; Psalms 84:2; Hebrews 4:12), no human personality or existence is possible if there is even one without the other two. In the Greek, the term for soul is *psuche* meaning, "the breath, and breath of life." It is that part of the human personality in which the mind, will, and emotions are both housed and centered. It is this part, the *psuche*, which frames most of the discussion and teaching of this book, although as you will see, what is stored in the soul has everything to do with what we do with our flesh bodies and our spirits.

In distinguishing the three parts for greater clarification, take note of 1 Corinthians 6 where the Apostle Paul calls attention to the flesh part of our triune nature by warning that fornication is the one sin that a man or woman commits against their own body. A second component, the soul, is what David is referring to in the 23rd Division of Psalms when he prays that the Lord would "restore" his soul — intimating that the soul can be fragmented (or somehow damaged) and would therefore be in need of restoration. (In understanding that the emotions, mind and will are housed in the soul, it is important from that point to understand that this "fragmentation" of the soul occurs as a result of anything that disquiets us such as trauma or tragedy, anything that causes depression or oppression, or anything that destabilizes our sense of well-being.)

We see yet a final distinction of the spirit (*pneuma*) as differing from the body or the soul in John 4:23, where Jesus explains to the woman at the well that it is with our spirit-by the assistance and guidance of the Holy Spirit — that we worship God (also Philippians 3:3), and which is "quickened" at the new birth experience. Clearly, the weight of scripture points to the significant potential of each part.

At the fall of man, the soul was corrupted as a result of sin, and became subservient to the whims and lusts of the flesh. The Apostle Paul explains that this war in our flesh is waged because of our constant struggle to keep the soul renewed after the things of God.

> *And be renewed in the spirit of your mind; And that Ye put on the new man, which after God is created in righteousness and true holiness.*
> *Ephesians 4:23, 24*

The soul must be conditioned daily (1 Peter 2:11; 1 Corinthians 9:27) and compelled to submit to the work of the cross in our lives. This renewing of the soul, in concert with the spirit, empowers me to deal with the terribleness of the flesh. So destructive and hopeless is this wretched body of flesh, the only solution to its inherent weakness is that it be changed — it can never be converted. This means that the flesh can never be saved.

> *Behold, I shew you a mystery; We shall not all sleep, but we shall all be changed, In a moment, in the twinkling of an eye, at the last trump: for the trumpet shall sound, and the dead shall be raised incorruptible, and we shall be changed. For this*

*corruptible must put on incorruption, and this
mortal must put on immortality. So when this
corruptible shall have put on incorruption, and this
mortal shall have put on immortality, then shall be
brought to pass the saying that is written, Death is
swallowed up in victory. 1 Corinthians 15:51-54*

Thank God, as the Apostle Paul goes on to say, however, that through Jesus Christ our Lord, a new, and living way has been made for us as a solution to this vile body of death. Let's look at Romans 7:20-25.

*Now if I do that I would not, it is no more I that do it,
but sin that dwelleth in me. I find then a law, that,
when I would do good, evil is present with me. For I
delight in the law of God after the inward man: but I
see another law in my members, warring against
the law of my mind, and bringing me into captivity to
the law of sin which is in my members. O wretched
man that I am! Who shall deliver me from the body
of this death? I thank God through Jesus Christ our
Lord. So then with the mind I myself serve the law of
God; but with the flesh the law of sin.*

Note that in verses 23 and 25, that word for "mind" is nous meaning (from *Vine's Expository Dictionary*, page 408), "the new nature, which belongs to the believer by reason of the new birth, Romans 7:23,25 where it is contrasted with 'the flesh' the principles of evil which dominates fallen man." This war, as aptly described by the Apostle Paul, involves the delight I have for the law of God (his Word) which seeks to direct this inward man (my soul) after godly precepts — but is in an ongoing conflict with my members (my flesh). Notice that the Apostle explains that one of our chief problems is that sin has its habitation in our members (the eyes, the nose, the hands, associations, etc.)

As this is the focal point of our struggles to live godly, clearly, as the Apostle so eloquently states, we need a deliverer from this body which is the habitation of eternal and physical death. Thank God that Jesus is become our salvation and great Deliverer. He makes it possible for us to break with the slavery caused by the lusts of this flesh. To appropriate deliverance from this body of death, a vigilant cleansing of the soul must occur daily through the washing of the Word (1 Peter 2:23; John 15:3).

How the Soul Gets Tied Up

At this point you can better understand why your soul keeps you in so much hot water. Because it is the seat of the emotions, mind, and will, every offense (perceived or real), trauma, and emotional scar, gets lodged there. Since we most often fail to continually cleanse and renew it with vigor and discipline, it is constantly vulnerable to the daily assault of our senses — wanting to dictate at a subconscious level, what will be forgiven and what will be saved for future reference. In understanding this, it is equally important to understand that part of our difficulty as children of light, is that for the most part we don't know that the soul absolutely requires that we cleanse it daily with the Word. Herein lies the greatest danger regarding our ignorance of the soul.

The soul gets tied up in matters (and people) which no longer affect our present lives. And yet, there they are like ghosts — mere shadows of things which no longer have substance or texture. We can't run from them because just a fragrance or the snatch of a faded memory can bring old traumas back fresh as if they occurred just a moment ago. We can't seem to forget them, because the memories of the hurts are there to taunt us as if to forget them would mean that they might happen again. We can't hide from them because even when life is good, and it seems like its okay to trust again, those old dead things linger around the edges of our emotions and swoop down on us at un-expectant moments — raining on the parades of life.

Visualize these issues which tie up the soul as skin layers of an onion. You can peel back one layer, but it only exposes something deeper and more insidious. These layers of the soulish realm become difficult to separate into separate, distinct events, because the root of any soul tie is always deeper than what is apparent. For example, a relationship soul tie may be deeper than just the two people involved. A woman whose heart has been broken by a man may have difficulty forgiving that man from the heart because of an unresolved issue with her father. In such a case, just severing the soul tie with the man is never enough. The soul is tied so intricately to so many let downs and hurts, that an issue which strengthens one tie may get entangled with an altogether different soul tie — the one having everything to do with the other — and yet either having very little to do with the other in terms of time, place, or thing.

No wonder Jesus told us that forgiveness is not possible unless it happens in the recesses of the heart (Matthew 18:35). It is there that we store recordings and images and scar tissue and our private brokenness, and even our errors which were long-ago forgiven by God. Is it no wonder the Word warns,

> *Keep thy heart with all diligence, for out of it are the issues of life. Proverbs 4:23*

Can We Talk?

When you stop and think about what you've gone through in your life, and the whole awfulness of it all, it can be quite daunting to think of a life without the past pain. You need to remember that your Creator had a plan for your life before you were even conceived in the womb. His perfect plan included a blessing for every crisis you would ever face. You were destined to succeed.

Having a better understanding of the complexities of your soul should not in any way dissuade you from the task at hand. Although you have many issues, unsettled in the secret crevices of your soul, you have a Lord who knows all, sees all, and is ready to face those issues with you. Take his courage and rest in his strength. It is so very important that as this book increases your understanding on the subject of soul ties, that you not feel overwhelmed about where you are and what it will take to take hold of deliverance. Are you bold enough to think that it may be simpler than you think? Let me prove it.

John's gospel, chapter 8, includes a snapshot in time and place concerning a woman who was caught in the sin of adultery. The Bible says, most candidly, "the very act" — or shall we rather point out that this is what her accusers said.

> *And the scribes and Pharisees brought unto him a woman taken in adultery; and when they had set her in the midst, They say unto him, Master, this woman was taken in adultery, in the very act. Now Moses in the law commanded us, that such should be stoned: but what sayest thou? And again he stooped down, and wrote on the ground. And they which heard it, being convicted by their own conscience, went out one by one, beginning at*

> *the eldest, even unto the last: and Jesus was left*
> *alone, and the woman standing in the midst. When*
> *Jesus had lifted up himself, and saw none but the*
> *woman, he said unto her, Woman, where are those*
> *thine accusers? hath no man condemned thee? She*
> *said, No man, Lord. And Jesus said unto her,*
> *Neither do I condemn thee: go, and sin no more.*

You see, sometimes our own worst accuser is the person we look at in the mirror everyday. Do you understand why I say this? It is because when we honor the Lord by repenting of our sins — no matter how disgusting, or how degrading those sins might be, Jesus silences the accusers in our lives. One by one, from the oldest accusation of past indiscretion, to the most recent, Jesus will silence them all — down to the very last man (or woman).

When you reject absolution and pardon, you demonstrate a profound lack of wisdom and understanding about the Cross. There is no amount of guilt or self-punishment that you can muster up that will sufficiently pay the sin-debt you owe. That is why we stand daily in need of a Savior. He then stands between us and those that would keep us in bondage to our own foolishness. Only he is worthy to do so. Only he can shut their mouths and send them slithering away. Only he can turn and look at us without condemnation and without chiding, and say, "Neither do I condemn thee. Go, and sin no more."

His "GO" means just what it says. It means you are free, you are set at liberty. It means your bill is paid in full. You could receive volumes of books on walking free of the condemnation of old sin and not benefit from them one bit if you really don't know Jesus as your Savior and Redeemer. Knowing about him is hardly sufficient — you must know *Him*. You must personally know him as the Lord who gives multiple chances for you to begin anew, even for the same sin. Yes... you read me right. He is the Lord who will forgive you over and over again for the same mess you committed umpteen times. Each day, he is ready to dip into a fresh new barrel of mercy for you and I. But it requires a major shift in your thinking... from one who stands guilty to one who stands in absolute pardon.

> *And I said, My strength and my hope is perished from the LORD: Remembering mine affliction and my misery, the wormwood and the gall. My soul hath them still in remembrance, and is humbled in me. This I recall to my mind, therefore have I hope. It is of the LORD's mercies that we are not consumed, because his compassions fail not. They are new every morning: great is thy faithfulness. The LORD is my portion, saith my soul; therefore will I hope in him. Lam 3:18-24*

Make no mistake about it. It may run contrary to your religious philosophy, but he is the God who restores a just man seven times for the same wrong (Proverbs 24:16). Does this "seven" mean literally seven and no more? On the eighth time, there would be no further place of repentance? NO! Seven is the number of divine completion... it indicates that whatever number of times it takes for you to get it in your spirit that Christ has redeemed you from the power and foothold of sin, that's what he is willing to provide.

> *Giving thanks unto the Father, which hath made us meet to be partakers of the inheritance of the saints in light: Who hath delivered us from the power of darkness, and hath translated us into the kingdom of his dear Son: In whom we have redemption through his blood, even the forgiveness of sins. Colossians 1:12-14*

If you can just remember that no matter how deep the pockets of trauma in your soul, that Christ ever lives to make intercession for you (Hebrews 7:25). Where are your accusers? Who are your accusers? It requires a major shift in your own thinking. Although your accusers are all gone (that is what Christ does when he pardons us), it is still possible to live the balance of your days thinking, reacting, and sounding like a victim.

Applying What You Have Learned

1. Write down three things you learned from this chapter that you did not understand about the soul part of man.

2. As a result of what you have learned in this chapter, what change needs to take place in your heart and mind before you read further in this book?

3. What will be the consequence if you refuse to change, or are unwilling to make steps which will bring about change?

4. To successfully bring change in your life, what covenant will you make with the Holy Spirit (he is your Helper and Comforter) so that without a doubt you will overcome the issue at hand? Please write it here or some place private which you can refer back to frequently.

5. Memorize this verse of scripture before going on to Chapter Two:

> For in that he himself hath suffered being tempted,
> he is able to succour them that are tempted.
> Hebrews 2:18

Chapter Two

Defining What a Soul Tie Is

The Strength of a Soul Tie is in the Joining

In the broadest definition possible, a "soul tie" is the joining or bonding between two or more persons through the doorway of the soul. However, a person can also have a soul tie with the world, with an organization or because of an association, or even with a demonic spirit. Again, the joining has occurred through the doorway of the individual's soul. Consider a couple of things in understanding what a soul tie is. First, some soul ties are sanctioned by God and are therefore *holy soul ties*. In contrast, some forms of joining or bonding are forbidden by God and can therefore produce *unholy soul ties*. This primarily results from the violation of God-ordained legal boundaries in the area of relationships and covenants.

Covenant Soul Ties

There are various and sometimes complex ways in which soul ties become fixed. One way in which a soul tie is formed is through *covenant relationship* expressed between two people. The simplest example is a close friendship; a weightier example is a marriage. The soul tie of marriage is perhaps the most sacred, because it is ratified by God Himself who then also becomes a party to the covenant (Malachi 2:14). Other examples include the shepherd to sheep covenant, a fellowship of churches, or a fellowship of believers.

Fornication Soul Ties

A different way in which a soul tie is formed is through *sexual intimacy*. Let's take a look at 1 Corinthians 6:15-20.

> *Know ye not that your bodies are the members of Christ? Shall I then take the members of Christ, and make them the members of an harlot? God forbid. What? Know ye not that he which is <u>joined</u> to an harlot is one body? For two, saith he, shall be one flesh. But he that is joined unto the Lord is one spirit. Flee fornication. Every sin that a man doeth is without the body; but he that committeth fornication sinneth against his own body. What? Know ye not that your body is the temple of the Holy Ghost which is in you, which ye have of God, and ye are not your own? For ye are bought with a price: therefore glorify God in your body, and in your spirit, which are God's.*

There is something quite illuminating in this portion of scripture which is hidden on first reading. In that 16th verse, that word "join" is *kollao* in the original Greek. Now take a look at Ephesians 5:31.

> *For this cause shall a man leave his father and his mother, and shall be <u>joined</u> unto his wife, and they two shall be one flesh.*

That word "join" in Ephesians 5:31 is *proskollao* in the original Greek. It is a strengthened form of the word used in 1 Corinthians 6:16. Did you get it? The same Greek root word that describes the oneness between a husband and a wife is the same root as the word which describes the oneness which occurs between two people who are sexually intimate, but not married. This "oneness" which occurs through the sin of fornication is illegal in the spirit realm, because it violates the sacred boundaries which God has established governing sexual intimacy.

Soul ties which occur through sexual intimacy outside of marriage, can wreck havoc on a man or woman's future relationship with the spouse of covenant. Repentance is only a part of it. Former soul ties of fornication must be severed in the authority of the Name of Jesus, or they are retained.

Soul Ties produced through Oaths

Yet another type of soul tie occurs through verbal agreements or oaths. This is one of those touchy issues, because the people of God have made vows and oaths to so many secret fraternities, secular organizations and private societies, that it has become a "pet" sin in the body of Christ. The error in the Body of Christ with respect to oaths and covenants is great and must truly injure the very heart of God. Let me give you an example for clarification. Look at this portion of scripture taken from 1 Samuel 20:11-17.

> *And Jonathan said unto David, Come, and let us go out into the field. And they went out both of them into the field. And Jonathan said unto David, O Lord God of Israel, when I have sounded my father about tomorrow any time, or the third day, and behold, if there be good toward David, and I then send not unto thee, and shew it thee; the Lord do so and much more to Jonathan: but if it please my father to do thee evil, then I will shew it thee, and send thee away, that thou mayest go in as he hath been with my father. And thou shalt not only while yet I live shew me the kindness of the Lord, that I die not: but also thou shalt not cut off thy kindness from my house for ever: no, not when the Lord hath cut off the enemies of David every one from the face of the earth. So Jonathan made a*

*covenant with the house of David, saying, Let the
Lord even require it at the hand of David's
enemies. And Jonathan caused David to swear
again, because he loved him: for he loved him as
he loved his own soul.*

You will notice that Jonathan and David made an oath
or covenant between each other that affected their *houses*.
Do you understand that when they joined their *houses*
together that more than they were involved? They actually
set in motion something which impacted their personal destinies, the destinies of their children, and even their children's children. They went so far as to bind even the enemies of David to the covenant agreement between them. The
vow they took had a powerful impact in the spirit realm.
Had the covenant been broken by David, who outlived
Jonathan, the houses of both men would have been trou-
bled. The Living Bible has an interesting paraphrase of
verse 16.

*So Jonathan made a covenant with the family of
David, and David swore to it with a terrible curse
against himself and his descendants, should he
be unfaithful to his promise.*

Whenever you enter into covenant agreement with an
organization, an association, a secret society, or whatever,
you bring your *house* and that house into a very spiritual
joining (or oneness) which has far-reaching, perhaps dangerous consequences. Not only that, but your covenant
agreement with an organization or association, means that
you bring yourself and your family under everything that
the organization/association stands for... good or evil.

You should even be careful of how you join or covenant
with religious organizations. Just because an organization
refers to God in its articles of incorporation, doesn't mean
that it is submitted to the Lordship of His Son, Jesus, and

committed to seeing his Kingdom established here on earth. Some of the fringe, racial supremist groups that promote violence and racial hatred are enough proof of this — their philosophy actually asserts that their activities are done in the Name of Christ.

> *Be not unequally yoked together with unbelievers: for what fellowship hath righteousness with unrighteousness? And what communion hath light with darkness? 2 Corinthians 6:14*

Broken and idolatrous vows carry long-term generational penalties, which is why scripture warns us about making any at all. Isn't it incredible that such a small member like our tongues can get us into so much hot water with God (James 3:5,6)? God has warned us that we should refrain from vows and oaths which bind our souls. Look at yet another passage of scripture which deals with the issue, which is Matthew 5:33-37.

> *Again, ye have heard that it hath been said by them of old time, Thou shalt not forswear thyself, but shalt perform unto the Lord thine oaths: but I say unto you, swear not at all; neither by heaven; for it is God's throne: nor by the earth; for it is his footstool: neither by Jerusalem; for it is the city of the great King. Neither shalt thou swear by thy head, because thou canst not make one hair white or black. But let your communication be, yea, yea; nay, nay: for whatsoever is more than these cometh of evil.*

Isn't that last verse interesting? The Word doesn't say that anything more than "yes" or "no" produces evil, it says that anything more than "yes" or "no" comes from an evil source. As a God-fearing society, we no longer have baal gods and groves in the high places where demon gods were once worshiped and adored, but modern-day idolatry is alive and well! People are still bowing their knees to demon gods in secret.

Soul Ties of Unforgiveness

We seldom think of soul ties developing as a result of unforgiveness, bitterness or hatred; but they are in fact, some of the most potent. In Matthew 18:32-35, a little known passage of scripture is often overlooked when there are teachings or sermons about unforgiveness.

> *Then his lord, after that he had called him, said unto him, O thou wicked servant, I forgave thee all that debt, because thou desiredst me: Shouldest not thou also have had compassion on thy fellow servant, even as I had pity on thee? And his lord was wroth, and delivered him to the tormentors, till he should pay all that was due him. So likewise shall my heavenly Father do also unto you, if ye from your hearts forgive not every one his brother their trespasses.*

Clearly, we are commanded to forgive, and are told quite frankly in Matthew 6:15, that unless we forgive, the Father will not forgive us.

> *But if ye forgive not men their trespasses, neither will your Father forgive your trespasses.*

Matthew 18 brings out quite another bit of information which should be just as frightening. That 34th verse tells us about a man being turned over to tormentors because he refused to forgive a debt. That 35th verse states unequivocally that, likewise, our gracious, loving, and merciful heavenly Father will actually turn us over to the tormentors (demons) if we fail to forgive.

Because the soul is the seat of the emotions, mind, and will, when you forgive someone from the heart, you release yourself from a soul tie with the individual who hurt you. Refusing to forgive, ties you or bonds you to the individual in an unholy way. This is often why people can replay old injuries like broken records in their minds for years and years after an injury is long past. It is because the sin of unforgiveness forges a soul tie with the victim and the one who caused the harm. The individual who committed the harm may even be dead and smoldering in their grave, but the tie is retained until forgiveness — from the heart — takes place.

Bloodline Soul Ties

The soul tie which exists between parents and their children are, of course, holy and therefore sanctioned by God. This type of soul tie, moreover, can be just as strong in a natural bloodline as in a spiritual bloodline as would be evident between persons who are in a mentoring and training relationship. An example of this was the relationship that existed between Elijah and Elisha. In a parent to child bloodline relationship, God considers a child produced through the covenant relationship of marriage, to be clean from conception. Adoptive parents, long-term foster parents, grandparents, and godparents — to a lessor extent — may also experience the tender bonds of parental bloodline soul ties.

When a parent crosses legally prohibited sexual boundaries which God places between parents and children, distinct, unholy soul ties between them are formed which are altogether unholy and perverse. This occurs even between children and relatives in a family bloodline. It can set generational curses of disease, sickness, deformity, birth defects, mental illness, and a host of other demonic strongholds in motion in a family line from generation to generation. The holy tie is eviscerated, giving rise to the unholy tie which then allows demons to enter and destroy the mental and physical well-being of a family to the fourth and fifth generations. We also describe this as giving "legal ground" to demons.

Yet another example occurs when a baby or child dies through sudden, untimely death, or through miscarriage, still birth, abortion, or what have you. Mothers who hold their newly-deceased infants bond with the child in a manner which the secular and medical profession considers giving "closure", but which forges powerful soul ties with the dead. God intended that death act as a natural severing of holy soul ties. When we grieve abnormally or in a prolonged manner for a deceased child, the soul tie with the dead child will produce all kinds of oppression for the grieving parents.

Further, the oppression fragments the soul of the living. A deliverance minister should never consider prolonged grieving as normal. It is completely abnormal and is a sure sign that a soul tie has been retained with the dead. The parental soul tie with that child needs to be severed in the Name of Jesus.

Finally, and on a different order, parents need to understand that God designed the marriage relationship to stand prominent to the parent/child relationship. Scripture (Ephesians 5:31) dictates that a man leave his mother and father and cleave to his wife.

> For this cause shall a man leave his father and mother, and shall be joined unto his wife, and they shall be one flesh.

Therefore, adult parents can actually set ungodly things in motion when they insist upon intruding into their adult children's marriages with their opinions and hidden agendas. The parent-child soul tie must become secondary to the husband/wife soul tie once children are emancipated and enter into the covenant relationship of marriage with a spouse.

Soul Ties with the Dearly Departed

As stated earlier, God intended that death serve as a natural severing for soul ties which are holy. For example, the scriptures indicate very clearly that a spouse who loses their mate in death is free — even encouraged to be joined to another (1 Timothy 5: 11). At the point at which the spouse of covenant dies, the surviving spouse is considered "unmarried". The blood covenant of marriage no longer binds the living to the dead. Grief, of course, is natural and to be expected. Prolonged grief, however, where a spouse or anyone else is concerned, is neither healthy nor spiritually acceptable.

Prolonged, morose grief in nearly all cases is a sure indication that a soul tie with the dead is retained. Clearly, maintaining a soul tie with one whom is deceased is not emotionally or physically productive. The scriptures indicate that the dead have no more portion in this natural life. Worse, those who are living can place absolutely no hope or further future plans in the generations of the dead.

> *For to him that is joined to all the living there is hope: for a living dog is better than a dead lion. For the living know that they shall die: but the dead know not anything, neither have they any more a reward; for the memory of them is forgotten. Also their love, and their hatred, and their envy, is now perished; neither have they any more a portion forever in anything that is done under the sun.*
> *Ecclesiastes 9:4-6*

For our understanding, Jesus gave us even greater clarification on the fact that death severs the marriage covenant

19

in Matthew 22:23-30 when the Sadducees tried to test him on the issue of the resurrection.

> *The same day came to him the Sadducees, which say that there is no resurrection, and asked him, Saying, "Master, Moses said, If a man die, having no children, his brother shall marry his wife, and raise up seed unto his brother. Now there were with us seven brethren: and the first, when he had married a wife, deceased, and having no issue, left his wife unto his brother: likewise the second also, and the third, unto the seventh. And last of all the woman died also. Therefore in the resurrection whose wife shall she be of the seven? For they all had her. Jesus answered and said unto them, Ye do err, not knowing the Scriptures, nor the power of God. For in the resurrection they neither marry, nor are given in marriage, but are as the angels of God in heaven.*

Admittedly, the loss of a soul mate or a loved one through death is both devastating and can be life shattering. Refusing to sever the soul tie, however, means that healing cannot take place. Very often, there is unfinished business (for example, cruel words that should never have been spoken — or kind words that should have been spoken but weren't) that holds the soul tie intact. Sometimes the unfinished business is that the surviving individual is angry because they feel that their loved one left them too soon or without sufficient time to prepare for their death. This does much to prolong the grieving process and can cripple an otherwise productive life from continuing. Knowing how and when to let go of a loved one who dies, is as important as freeing ourselves of soul ties which God considers unholy if we persist in retaining them.

Can We Talk?

When you started the book, you may have started with the erroneous ideas that fornication soul ties were the only ones there were, or that all soul ties are unholy. I have heard teachers of the Word use the word "soul tie" as if it were a dirty word. Now that you understand that some soul ties are considered holy by God, has your understanding increased about why the unholy ties are unholy?

At a minimum you should understand that it is sin which leads to the development of a soul tie which is unholy — and it is this spiritually illegal joining which makes absolute severance so difficult — but certainly not impossible. The first soul tie there ever was is the God-sanctioned soul tie of holy matrimony. How then can all soul ties be unholy?

Some of you stumbled in chapter Two when we discussed the problem God has with the vows and covenants you took with perhaps benevolent, secular organizations. Others of you just about fell over at the suggestion of severing the soul tie you have with your deceased child or spouse. Do you understand that in both instances we are counseling you to sever covenant with organizations and persons who are dead? I stumbled over this last one myself for almost a year when someone who was very close to me died suddenly. I felt that severing the soul tie would be an act of disloyalty. How can you be disloyal to someone who is dead? I discovered that the best way of honoring his memory was to release him in my heart and spirit so that I could benefit from the treasures he had planted in my life. Prolonged grief and the presence of what had developed as an unholy soul tie stopped me from being able to do that.

Stop thinking that releasing your still-born will hurt them further. In that place called Paradise where they now live and thrive, no disease, sickness, ill-feeling, or even the love you have for them can touch them or move them. They are completely unaffected by the things of this realm. As for you the living, should you refuse to sever that tie, you will live the balance of your days stunted in that area of loving in your heart. It will become mummified and not yield to hope or the promise of springtime.

What you are doing when you tell yourself that you just cannot bring yourself to sever the soul tie is actually very self-centered and should not be viewed as normal. Stop looking inward at what the loss has done to you and how it makes you feel, and truly love and honor the one who now lives in eternity. Forgive them for dying and causing you to feel so bad. Stop looking inward and choose life! If you live a life that is pleasing to Christ, have no fear, you will join them shortly.

> *Man that is born of a woman is of few days, and*
> *full of trouble. Job 14:1*

$\mathcal{A}pplying$ $\mathcal{W}hat$ $\mathcal{Y}ou$ $\mathcal{H}ave$ $\mathcal{L}earned$

1. What did you learn from this chapter about soul ties? Jot a few things down.

2. As you read, the Holy Spirit convicted you about some things that you will need to repent for, and even change in your life. What were those matters? List them here.

3. If you choose not to sever the soul ties which God considers unholy, nothing much may happen in the natural realm. What, if any, consequences will/has happened in the spirit realm? Having reflected on that sobering conclusion, are you in any way convicted about bringing change? What change and when?

4. Have you severed soul ties with loved ones who are now deceased? What evidence do you see?

5. Memorize this portion of scripture before going on to Chapter Three:

    From the end of the earth will I cry unto thee, when my heart is overwhelmed: lead me to the rock that is higher than I. Ps 61:2

Chapter Three

The Soul Tie of Marriage

*"For this cause shall a man leave his father and
his mother, and shall be joined unto his wife, and
they two shall be one flesh." Ephesians 5:31*

Covenants and Oaths

The soul tie of marriage is based on covenant and is not
only one of the most sacred, but is the first example of
covenant that we have depicted in the scriptures. In mod-
ern day word usage, we think of "making" a covenant with
someone or something as the act which binds us to that
thing. Biblically, a covenant is not considered something
that you make or break, as such. Rather, you cut (*karat* is
the Hebrew term) a covenant as a form of establishing a
sacred vow or trust. In addition, biblically, once a covenant
was *cut*, it was accompanied by a sign and/or attested to by
witnesses.

There are some interesting examples of this in scripture.
In several instances, (Ezra 10: 19, Lamentations 5:6, and
Ezekiel 17:1), a covenant was ratified when one offered their
hand to another as a sign of the binding nature of the agreement. In Ruth 4:7-11, we have the example where Naomi's
near kinsman loosened his shoe to secure the agreement. In
1 Samuel 18:3,4, Jonathan stripped himself of his garments
as a sign of his covenant with David. Yet another example
occurs in 2 Chronicles 13:5, where salt was used to seal a
covenant agreement.

Covenants were not only binding on the part of those
who made them, but on those who were represented *in* the
vow agreement. Hence, any breach of the covenant on the

part of the primary agents or their descendants resulted in great disaster. A classic example of the tragedy of a broken covenant on a man's descendants is found in 2 Samuel 21:1-9.

In this biblical account, we learn that a Canaanite people called the Gibeonites had tricked Joshua and the chosen people of God into believing they were a people from a far away country journeying through Canaan. When their trickery was discovered, it was too late. The Israelites had cut a covenant with them which spared their lives. The covenant agreement allowed them to live, provided they performed the tasks of slaves (Joshua 9:21).

According to 2 Samuel 21, in the years following the death of Joshua and the Israelites who agreed to the pact, King Saul broke the covenant of peace with the descendants of the Gibeonites. Years later, during the reign of King David, a three year famine blighted the land. Fortunately, David was a man who knew his God intimately. In desperation, King David sought the face of the Lord to learn the source of the terrible curse on the land. David learned that God's wrath had been kindled against the 'bloodthirsty house' of Saul for his breach of the Gibeonite covenant — which had been duly established under Joshua.

> *During the reign of David, there was a famine for three successive years; so David sought the face of the LORD. The Lord said, It is on account of Saul and his blood-stained house; it is because he put the Gibeonites to death. 2 Samuel 21:1*

In order to turn the curse, David allowed the Gibeonites to hang seven of Saul's descendants (2 Samuel 21:9). Can you imagine having to bear the guilt of an oath which your ancestor made and broke before you were even born? Imagine if you will that there is a breach in such a covenant that you *are* aware of. How will you turn aside the curse which broken oaths and covenants set in motion? How will you appease God for a rash vow spoken from the mouth of an ancestor who foolishly bound you to fulfillment of their oath? For that matter, how will you appease your adversary who gains legal entry into your life and circumstances as a result of the rash vows taken by your forefathers? Why don't you take a moment right now and thank God for his grace and mercy.

Clearly, the conditions of such covenants unfairly bind the interests of unknowing descendants. The scripture is clear, however, that even if a covenant vow is unknown by a man's descendants, it is still binding in the natural and spiritual realms. Let's look at two different renderings of Galatians 3:15. From the KJV, it reads,

> *Brethren, I speak after the manner of men; Though it be but a man's covenant, yet if it be confirmed, no man disannulleth, or added thereto.*

From the NIV, the same portion of scripture reads,

> *Brothers, let me take an example from everyday life. Just as no one can set aside or add to a human covenant that has been duly established, so it is in this case.*

In understanding the awesome repercussions for binding oneself to a covenant agreement and then breaking it, it is now easier to understand the insolubility of the most sacred of covenants, which is the marriage covenant. Before we move there, let's give final emphasis to two very important points. First, when a person binds himself to an oath, he may unwittingly also bind his descendants as parties to the same agreement. Should they, or their descendants, knowingly or unknowingly break the terms of the covenant, the consequences will most certainly end in tragedy. Finally, broken covenants are accompanied by a sign even as established covenants are accompanied by a sign. As we turn our attention to the soul tie of marriage, keep both points in mind.

The Marriage Covenant is Called the "Covenant of God"

Before we look at the first covenant of marriage described in scripture, let's first look at Malachi 2:14-17 which explains why marriage is considered the "Covenant of God."

> *Yet ye say, Wherefore? Because the Lord hath been witness between thee and the wife of thy youth, against whom thou hast dealt treacherously: yet is she thy companion, and the wife of thy covenant. And did not he make one? <u>Yet had he the residue of the spirit</u>. And wherefore one? That he might seek a godly seed. Therefore take heed to your spirit, and let none deal treacherously against the wife of his youth. For the Lord, the God of Israel, saith that he hateth putting away: for one covereth violence with his garment, saith the Lord of hosts: therefore take heed to your spirit, that ye deal not treacherously. Ye have wearied the Lord with your words. Yet ye say, Wherein have we wearied him? When ye say, Every one that doeth evil is good in the sight of the Lord, and he delighteth in them; or, Where is the God of judgment?*

Notice that when two people (a man and a woman) cut a covenant of matrimony, God as well as the heavenly host give witness to this most sacred of covenant vows. Take note of the underlined portion of the text above. Although the joining of marriage unites two flesh beings into one, God jealously joins the spirit of each of us to himself. 2 Corinthians 6:17 states unequivocally,

But he that is joined unto the Lord is one spirit.

It is yet important to understand that even if the two taking the vows are unbelievers, as long as they are male and female, it is the sacrament of marriage itself which is honored and considered holy by God.

> *Marriage is honorable among all, and the bed undefiled; but fornicators and adulterers God will judge. Hebrews 13:4*

The 14th verse of Malachi 2 bears closer examination. As the Lord Himself and Most Holy witnesses "between" the man and his wife, God declares the cutting of this peculiar covenant to be insoluble (except of course where fornication or death of one's spouse occurs — see Matthew 1:19; 19:3-9; 5:31, 32; 22:25,30). Look at the language of the text from Malachi 2:14:

> <u>Yet</u> *is she thy companion, and the wife of thy covenant.*

In this portion of Malachi, where the marriage covenant is referred to as the "Covenant of God," we gain an understanding that to enter into marital covenant with a spouse is to also enter into a marital covenant with God. In breaking marital covenant with a spouse, we also break covenant with God. As we have explained earlier, whenever an oath or covenant is duly established even by a human being or method, it cannot be annulled on a whim, neither can its influence be dismissed lightly. Can you now better understand why in most cases the act of divorcing a spouse (we will explain the proviso *"most"* in Chapter Four) is actually the breaking of covenant with God?

To "Cut" is to "Join"

As we have already explained, from a biblical point of view, a covenant is literally "cut", not made. As regards to marriage, the covenant is cut in the flesh of the man and enforced by the law of leaving and cleaving. The scriptures call it "joining." Look first at Mark 10:7-9:

> For this cause shall a man leave his father and mother, and <u>cleave</u> to his wife; and they twain shall be one flesh: so then they are no more twain, but one flesh. What therefore God hath joined together, let not man put asunder.

That word "cleave" is *kollao* in the Greek text, it means "to become cemented to." The law of leaving and cleaving, therefore, requires that a man (or woman) relegate the child-to-parent soul tie secondary to the marital tie. Second, notice again that word "joined" in verse 9. It is *sonzeugnumi* in the Greek text. It means to "yoke together in the flesh." Consider for a moment that throughout the Old and New Testaments that this expression of "two becoming one flesh" is always and in every case indicative of the peculiar marriage covenant. Herein lies the key to the mystery of what *really* happens when a man and a woman enter into the covenant of marriage. God cut the covenant in Adam's body that the woman might become possessor of his blood and partaker of his life.

As you hold on to the meaning of the word *sonzeugnumi*, which means "to yoke together in the flesh," ponder for a moment the impossibility (from a natural point of view) of two separate human beings becoming one flesh being. Yet, isn't this what God says occurs when two people cut the covenant of marriage? Is this figurative language? Let me show you that it is not figurative language — but is an actual and literal indication of what occurs in the marriage covenant. Let's now go back to the beginning, where the first covenant of marriage was cut. Genesis 2:20-25 reads as follows:

> *And Adam gave names to all cattle, and to the fowl of the air, and to every beast of the field; but for Adam there was not found an help meet for him. And the Lord God caused a deep sleep to fall upon Adam, and he slept: and he took one of his ribs, and closed up the flesh instead thereof; and the rib, which the Lord God had taken from man, made he a woman, and brought her unto the man. And Adam said, This is now bone of my bones, and flesh of my flesh: she shall be called Woman, because she was taken out of Man. Therefore shall a man leave his father and his mother, and shall cleave unto his wife: and they shall be one flesh. And they were both naked, the man and his wife, and were not ashamed.*

Did you notice the sequence of events that occurred before the woman was presented to the man by God? Look at it again. God always knows what he has in mind before he begins a thing. He deliberately did not go back to the ground when he created the woman. Instead, God put the man to sleep, cut him open, took one of the man's ribs and built up or sculpted the woman from the flesh and bones he had cut out of the man. In cutting the man thus so, God cut or *karat* the covenant of marriage supernaturally and divinely in the flesh of the male.

What is the significance of the rib? Some say that the location of the rib in the human anatomy — close to the heart, but at the side — makes it the logical area from which God chose to make himself a woman. The ribs are curved portions of flesh and bones which are located in the upper torso of the human body. In taking one of the man's ribs, God eternally made the man incomplete in the flesh — the medical establishment has, in fact, confirmed that a man is missing one rib.

Adam still had perfect unity with God the Father in spirit and in soul, but his flesh would be throughout all eternity incomplete. When you consider the whole of the human anatomy, what other area of the human body could God have taken a portion, and yet left enough intact from which to build another human being? The head? The lower torso? The legs? The upper torso provided a perfect symmetry of organs, vessels, and bones from which God could sculpt a separate and distinct being.

The Marriage Covenant is a Blood Covenant

In noting that God cut the man's flesh from which he then sculpted the woman, it is equally important to note that cutting involved a blood covenant. Biblically, blood covenants which were cut in the flesh were serious business. As with the Abrahamic covenant, blood covenants also covered descendants and carried a grim penalty when broken. Failure to observe the blood covenant of circumcision, which involved cutting the foreskin of every eight-day-old male, carried a spiritual penalty.

In Exodus 4:20-26, in an otherwise difficult to understand portion of scripture, the Lord was prepared to kill Moses because the first born son of Moses and Zipporah had not been properly circumcised (not entitled to the blessings included in the Abrahamic covenant). An uncircumcised Hebrew boy was considered cursed and his father was held accountable for the oversight — even if he was as important a personality as Moses!

What the blood covenant of marriage demonstrates is that a husband and wife are covenanted to God by blood first, and then secondarily to the man in his flesh. This two-fold sign of the strength of the marriage covenant, again, exemplifies the severe penalty that attaches when such a covenant as this is broken. When a man invokes the blood vow (covenant) of matrimony over his wife, he pledges his very life for her. This certainly casts a different light on Ephesians 5:28 when one looks at holy matrimony as a blood covenant — doesn't it?

> *So ought men to love their wives as their own bodies. He that loveth his wife loveth himself.*

Isn't it interesting that even as Christ loved and gave himself for the Church, that the New Covenant by which we are married to him, was instituted in his shed blood? The sharing of blood in covenant represents communion and fellowship. In Holy Communion, and as members of the Lord's Body, we drink the Lord's blood and eat his flesh (John 6:53-58) as evidence of our fellowship or marriage with him.

Remember that Greek word we looked at a bit earlier which means to "yoke together in the flesh"? Again, it is *sonzeugnumi.* In verses 20-25 of Genesis 2, notice that Adam and Eve literally became yoked together in the flesh. They were of one flesh — Adam's. Now notice Adam's declaration in verse 23, *"This is now bone of my bones, and flesh of my flesh..."* Having thus spoken, Adam speaks the first recorded marriage vow. God stands as his witness, and ultimately his judge. He not only agrees to accept the woman, but he agrees to cover her and shield her. At a most basic level then, marriage provides covering, protection, and divine sanction (favor).

What then, is the sign that God has ratified the marriage covenant? It appears in verses 24 and 25 of Genesis 2. When we recount the creative acts of God, we always forget one. You will notice that Adam and Eve are at first two distinct human beings — they are the first singles in the scripture. But then Adam speaks the marriage vow, invoking the covenant of matrimony. As he does so, God ratifies the covenant by *rejoining* (or reconciling) these two and making them one again — even while drawing a clear distinction between their genders. It is a completely different creative act. In a manner of speaking, in marriage, a man gets back what was taken from him in that deep sleep.

This is really a very rich portion of scripture with layers and layers of spiritual truth. We have missed it through the ages. Isn't it interesting that before God formed the woman, he declared the man to be alone (Genesis 2:18). Second, it was God who declared that the man needed help — and that no thing on the face of the earth which had already been created, could serve as an appropriate help meet for the man. Finally, it was God who declared that when a man is alone (in the single state) "it is not good." Since God took from the man what he intended to return to him only by means of the marriage covenant, he made it an impossibility for a man to ever be truly complete alone — that is, without a wife.

The Husband's Obligation to Love

The Holy Spirit, speaking through the mouth of the Apostle Paul, had a lot to say about the marriage relationship, specifically, how husbands and wives are to relate to each other. It bears noting in this excerpt from Ephesians 5:28:

> *So ought men to love their wives as their own bodies. He that loveth his wife loveth himself.*

A bold statement on first reading, indeed. But, when one considers that the marriage covenant is the "Covenant of God," ratified by God, and cut in the very flesh of the man, the injunction for the man to love his wife as his own body is clear. The wife, in fact, *is his body* — God rejoins the man and woman when the marriage covenant is cut, making them one flesh. If it sounds so simple, why does God have to command men to love their wives?

In Ephesians 5, that word for love is *agapao*. Sound familiar? Notice that it is not *phileo*, which is translated love also, but means "tender affection." That term for love used in Ephesians 5:28, *agapao*, expresses deep, constant love, not affection! It is reverential love. It is not based on how a husband *feels* about his wife, nor is it based on her worthiness of his love. This kind of love, *agapao*, values and esteems. It is unselfish, and it seeks foremost to serve. Now that deserves some momentary consideration! It also bears noting, however, that wives more often than not place a greater weight on a show of affection from their husbands, and less on the service or provision that a husband bestows!

Think how often spouses who are headed to divorce court express their desire for a dissolution of the marriage covenant based on the fact that they no longer *feel* love for each other. The Word of God is clear that a husband is expected — even commanded — to *agapao* his wife in a constant, no-conditions-attached, manner. It is the way that Christ loves his own bride, which is the Church.

The Husband's Spiritual Authority

Admittedly, the man's level of accountability is greatest in the marriage covenant. The full weight of scripture demonstrates clearly that it is the man that God ultimately holds responsible for the failure of a marriage. The reasons for this can be traced back to the Adamic curse.

> *Unto the woman he said, I will greatly multiply thy sorrow and thy conception; in sorrow thou shalt bring forth children; <u>and thy desire shall be to thy husband, and he shall rule over thee</u>. Genesis 3:16*

There are Old and New Testament scriptural references which point to the scriptural authority of the husband over the wife. One of the earliest examples we can provide of the husband's exalted position is in Numbers 30 where the Mosaic law gave him the power to cancel any contracts or agreements made by his wife within a day's time (provided he was aware that his wife had made a contract). Arguably, although we are no longer under the law, a husband still has the spiritual authority to cancel contracts made by his wife without his agreement.

Some will certainly argue that this provision of the Mosaic law is no longer tenable, but when the Apostle Paul addressed the issue in 1 Corinthians 11:3,9 and 10, he had this to say on the subject,

> But I would have you know, that the head of every man is Christ; and the head of the woman is the man; and the head of Christ is God. Neither was the man created for the woman; but the woman for the man. For this cause ought the woman to have power on her head because of the angels.

Nontraditional family relationships abound in our society. However, the lines of spiritual authority which are established by God are clearly delineated. We may argue about what a socially acceptable family unit is, but God's opinion is clear and unwavering. The man is accountable to God, the woman is accountable to her husband, and children are accountable to their parents. Any act of rebellion to this God-sanctioned order in the family will result in any number of curses and plagues visited upon that household.

This obviously means that a husband who willingly abdicates his place of headship in the family incurs the wrath of God by leaving his family uncovered. By the same token, the man who knows and appreciates the extensive level of authority which God has afforded him as the head of his family, has the power to do much to block the enemy's attacks on his wife and children. Unfortunately, the issue of authority is little taught, except as regards the shepherd-to-sheep relationship. Unless and until the Body of Christ comes into a clearer understanding that authority provides <u>covering</u>, the attitude held by the world that any kind of family unit is just as good as the next, will continue to permeate the thinking of the Church as well.

Finally, as we pointed out earlier, as long as a woman's husband is alive, he retains authority or headship over her in the spirit realm. This, perhaps the strongest soul tie there is, has far reaching consequences for the couple who enters into marriage lightly or for the wrong reasons. As we will explain later, God does not recognize a writ of divorce unless it legally and spiritually meets his specifications. What this means then, is that unless the soul tie of marriage is severed to God's liking, a woman's living "ex" husband(s) still retains his authority over her, though she be married to another (Romans 7:3).

Applying What You Have Learned

1. Explain why the covenant of marriage is one of the most sacred.

2. What are some of the consequences of a broken covenant on a man's/woman's descendants? Understanding this, what do you believe are the consequences of a broken marital covenant on their descendants?

3. Why did God make man the head of the wife? What does this headship have to do with authority and covering?

4. The shedding of blood ratifies (seals) a covenant in a spiritual manner. Where is the shedding of blood in the marriage covenant? How does a man's confession during matrimony that the woman is "bone of his bone and flesh of his flesh" bear this out?

5. Why did Christ compare his love and devotion to the church, to the love a man should have for his wife? Where is the comparison? Give a scriptural basis for your answer.

Chapter Four

Divorce, a Soul Tie Retained

"What therefore God hath joined together, let not man put asunder." Mark 10:9

Seeing Divorce as Sin

In this portion of scripture, Jesus' words can literally be taken to mean that what God has yoked together in the flesh, don't let any man dis-joint it! I shudder to think of the spiritual impact of this declaration on the lives of men and women who are divorce lawyers and judges. It should also provide a very sober warning to any person whose presence so captivates a married individual, that such an individual is either able to separate a husband from his wife, or cause that married person to break their marital vows. No good thing will come of an affair, and whatever is sown, shall sooner or later get reaped.

For years, the Pentecostal church taught that divorce will surely land you in hell. Some denominations still teach that a divorced person cannot even be saved. The scriptural basis of such an opinion is dubious, but there is basis for the strong line taken against it. Let me start by saying with earnest and without equivocation, God considers divorce to be sin (Mark 10:2,4,11-12; Matthew 5:31). It is probably the second most prevalent sin in the Body of Christ right now. (I happen to personally believe that idolatry is number one.)

It is so prevalent, in fact, that even the great men and women of God with international ministries are reluctant to call it for what it is. It is so rife throughout the Body, that some of our greatest generals of ministry are working on their second and third marriages. You are certainly not going to point your finger at something and condemn it if you are living in it.

Believe it or not, Jesus didn't have a whole bunch of *different* things to say about divorce. In searching the scriptures to examine his feelings about the subject, you will notice that he is quite consistent in expressing the same sentiment. In Matthew's gospel 5:32, these words are recorded,

> *But I say unto you, That whosoever shall put away his wife, saving for the cause of fornication, causeth her to commit adultery: and whosoever shall marry her that is divorced committeth adultery.*

In Mark's gospel, 10:11,12, Jesus is quoted a little differently, but you get the clear sense that he has not changed his perspective about the matter.

> *And he saith unto them, Whosoever shall put away his wife, and marry another, committeth adultery against her. And if a woman shall put away her husband, and be married to another, she committeth adultery.*

Notice several things from the text. First, if you'll reread it, you'll notice that as far as God is concerned, a man and a woman don't stop being married just because they have a piece of paper with the word "divorce" on it. Realize that the only way that Jesus could declare someone to be an adulterer who re-marries after divorcing their spouse, he would have to consider that person to still be married to the person they divorced. You follow me? On first reflection, it would seem that our meaning for adultery is different from God's — but not really.

We define an adulterer as someone who is married and has an affair outside of their marriage vows. We consider such a person to be someone who has broken their vows and in sexual sin. Now compare God's definition. He thinks that an adulterer is someone who is married, gets divorced, and marries somebody else. Or, in a different example, was single, and got married to someone who used to be married to someone else. How can we reconcile this gross difference in the way adultery is defined and viewed by God and us? We can't.

Clearly, God believes that an individual who remarries, is actually still married to the person they *first* married. Our society says that a person who is married to more than one person at a time is a polygamist. God says that a person who is married to a divorced person, or who remarries after divorce is a polygamist.

You say, but what about Old Testament figures who were married to more than one woman like Abraham, David, Lamech, Esau, Jacob, Gideon, Solomon, and Elkanah (to name just a few)? They were polygamists, yes, but you will notice that they provided for all of their wives and for the children of each of these wives. They didn't put one away in order to marry another. In Mark's gospel, chapter 10, in fact, when the Pharisees came to tempt Jesus with the whole issue, Jesus reminded them that Moses had given them the provision of divorce which permitted them to put away their wives, because of the hardness of their hearts.

The measure (bill of divorcement) wasn't just for the benefit of the husband, but it was also intended to protect women societally from being simply abandoned by their husbands. The bill of divorcement, at a minimum, released a woman so that she could marry another and be provided for. But as Jesus goes on to say in that passage from Mark 10:5-9, God never sanctioned divorce, because he intended that the joining between a man and wife in holy matrimony should be insoluble until death loosed them from their covenant vows.

The best clue to understanding why God's position is so strict and unbending toward the issue of divorce, is understanding that when God established the covenant of marriage (referred to in scripture as the *Covenant of God*), he cut the covenant of marriage in the man's flesh when he took the woman out of the man. The whole reason for the woman's being was for the man. This is why the Apostle Paul declares that a man should love his wife as his own body. She is his own body, as far as God is concerned.

> *Yet ye say, Wherefore? Because the Lord hath been witness between thee and the wife of thy youth, against whom thou has dealt treacherously: yet is she thy companion, and the wife of thy covenant. And did not he make one? Yet had he the residue of the spirit."* Malachi 2:15a

The Apostle Paul goes on to call marriage a "great mystery" and likens it to the joining of Christ to his Body, the Church.

> *For no man ever yet hated his own flesh; but nourisheth and cherisheth it, even as the Lord the church: for we are members of his body, of his flesh, and of his bones. For this cause shall a man leave his father and mother, and shall be joined unto his wife, and they two shall be one flesh. This is a great mystery: but I speak concerning Christ and the church. Ephesians 5:29-32*

Obviously, the covenant of marriage is so sacred and divine, that it should certainly not be entered into lightly. The Bible even indicates that in the last days as a sign of Jesus' imminent return, divorce would be rampant (Luke 17:26-30).

Fornication Revokes the Marriage Covenant

Admittedly, there may be grounds for divorce that God sanctions. While it is true that too often we look for "loopholes" in the Word of God when we fall short of its commandments and precepts, it may be so that not all marriages are ordained of God in the first place. When the Word talks of two people being joined by God, it is talking about two people who meet his requirements for the marriage covenant. In the same way that not just any contract is legally binding, not just any marriage between any two people can be considered alright with God.

The prototype that God established was a marriage between a man and a woman, who were willing parties to the covenant, of sound enough mind to assert the covenant vows rationally, and who were otherwise emancipated — which allowed them to be joined to each other. So to provide an example, a licensed and ordained minister could unite two men in marriage, but does God sanction such covenant? Do they meet the requirements? No in both instances.

What of spousal violence or abuse, or situations where one spouse fornicates outside of the covenant of marriage? Is such a marriage still insoluble from God's point of view? Let's look at what Jesus had to say about the issue of the marital vows being broken through sexual transgression.

> And I say unto you, Whosoever shall put away his wife, <u>except it be for fornication</u>, and shall marry another, committeth adultery: and whoso marrieth her which is put away doth commit adultery.
> Matthew 19:9

The words of Jesus would seem to indicate that marriage is considered binding on the two individuals who entered into the covenant agreement, unless fornication is involved. The standard he gives us is sexual impropriety, which results in an annulment of the marriage covenant. Hence, in this one instance at least, a spouse is free to terminate or annul the marital vows without the prohibition of remaining forever in the unmarried state. Since the marital vows would be considered violated, we would consider both persons "unmarried" or no longer married.

To state it a different way, since the Savior gives fornication as a justifiable reason (in God's sight) for divorce, the implication from the text is just as clear that the spouse who has been cheated on is *free* to remarry. In fact, they are encouraged to do so, in order to avoid falling into fornication themselves. In 1 Corinthians 7:8-10,15, the Apostle Paul who is usually very strict in his viewpoints, has this to say to a believer who divorces:

> *I say therefore to the unmarried and widows, It is good for them if they abide even as I. But if they cannot contain, let them marry: for it is better to marry than to burn. And unto the married, I command, yet not I, but the Lord, Let not the wife depart from her husband: But and if she depart, let her remain unmarried, or be reconciled to her husband: and let not the husband put away his wife. But if the unbelieving depart, let him depart. A brother or sister is not under bondage in such cases: but God hath called us to peace.*

Is it doctrinally correct to tell a young woman that because divorce is sin, God expects her to stay with a husband who physically and mentally abuses her? Some churches not only teach that the answer to this is yes, but give 1 Corinthians 7:8-10 as their foundation. What a gross misinterpretation of scripture, not to mention the fact that it is a contextual error. In no instance does the Savior or the Apostle Paul suggest that a man who violates God's commandment with respect to the way a husband is to treat his wife, is free to violate her with impunity (or with his fists!). In no place, does the Savior or the Apostle Paul even suggest that a wife or a husband who is victimized by spousal abuse should stay there and take it.

Clearly, if we look at the standard which the Savior gives us in making fornication the exception to God's prohibition against divorce, spousal abuse of any kind is a violation of the marriage covenant. If a man has a wife who refuses sexual intimacy with him decides to divorce her, is the sin that this wife has committed against her husband any less egregious than an act of adultery against him? Scripture plainly teaches that a married couple should not defraud or deny each other in sexual intimacy, and that further, they are to submit their bodies one to the other. It would appear, contextually, that the standard that the Savior raises as far as fornication being a violation of the marital covenant, in that one spouse offers his/her body to a "harlot" in adultery, would equally apply to a situation where one spouse refuses to submit their body to each other. Let's take one more look at Matthew 19:9 so that I can explain.

> *And I say unto you, Whosoever shall put away his wife, except it be for __fornication__, and shall marry another, committeth __adultery__: and whoso marrieth her which is put away doth commit adultery.*

Notice first that the Savior makes a distinction between fornication and adultery which means he sees the two acts in a different light than perhaps we do. The revelation is in the Greek meanings of the two terms; which may surprise you. The word *fornication* comes from the Greek word _porneia_ which includes a host of sexual sins and, by definition, includes adultery and incest as well. One more surprise with respect to the Greek term *porneia* is that it also includes the sin of idolatry. The term *adultery*, on the other hand, is _moichos_ in the original Greek. It means *"one who has unlawful sexual intercourse with the spouse of another"* (Luke 18: 11; 1 Corinthians 6:9; Hebrews 13:4; James 4:4).

In using the term *porneia*, the Savior is perhaps indicating that __any__ sexual sin against a spouse is justifiable grounds for divorce! This would include a spouse who refuses to submit to his/her spouse in sexual intimacy, or a spouse who commits the crime of incest against his/her child or near relative. *Fornication* is the broader term which encompasses all forms of sexual indiscretion. *Adultery* is the narrower term, speaking specifically to a married person who is sexually intimate with another person who is also married.

Let's now take a look at the way the Apostle Paul touched the issue in 1 Corinthians 7:2-5:

> *Nevertheless, to avoid fornication, let every man have his own wife, and let every woman have her own husband. Let the husband render unto the wife due benevolence: and likewise also the wife unto the husband. The wife hath no power of her own body, but the husband: and likewise also the husband hath no power of his own body, but the wife. Defraud ye not one the other, except it be with consent for a time, that ye may give yourselves to fasting and prayer; and come together again, that satan tempt you not for your incontinency.*

The marriage covenant includes spiritual and physical vows of commitment and submission to each other. A spouse is not under bondage to stay married to a person who has violated those vows. Although the Apostle Paul believed and taught that anyone loosed from marriage should stay unmarried, it is not clear that Jesus agreed with this standard. The Apostle does concede that not everybody can receive such a saying. If you can't, then clearly you should re-marry.

One thing is clear, divorce is sin except on the grounds of *porneia* (all forms of sexual indiscretion) or where a spouse has broken the marital vows in other abhorrent ways. The only remedy for the sin of divorce is repentance; and it doesn't hurt to repent even if you have justifiable cause. After all, repentance is a small price to pay for the mistake you made in marrying the wrong man or woman. Refusing to repent means that the sin goes unpardoned, which means that your children are doomed to reap the fruit of your sin for generations to come.

There is yet one more important reason why you must repent for the sin of divorce before you even think about the possibility of remarriage. A bill of divorce does not sever the soul tie of marriage! This occurs through the power of the cross and the blood of Jesus Christ, which frees us from the penalty of sin. Hence, unless you repent, you have no foundation upon which you can sever the soul tie of a previous marriage. Repentance brings pardon and absolution. You are then empowered, in the Name of Jesus, to sever that tie forever and be freed of any spiritual authority that your former spouse might try to exert over you because of it.

If, on the other hand, you divorced on the grounds of fornication or spousal abuse, you too need to sever the marriage covenant soul tie and declare any spiritual authority once held by your husband/wife over you to be canceled in the Name of Jesus.

Divorce Sets a Curse in Motion

As we explained in the chapter, "The Soul Tie of Marriage," one who breaks covenant with a spouse through divorce, has spiritually broken covenant with God. Why? Because the marriage covenant, as we have said, is the "Covenant of God." It bears such magnitude and power that God the Father modeled the new testament relationship of Christ to the Church from it.

There is yet another danger of breaking covenant with God through divorce, which is found in Ecclesiastes 5:4-6

> *When thou vowest a vow unto God, defer not to*
> *pay it; for he hath no pleasure in fools: pay that*

> *which thou has vowed. Better is it that thou*
> *shouldest not vow, than that thou shouldest vow*
> *and not pay. Suffer not thy mouth to cause thy*
> *flesh to sin; neither say thou before the angel, that*
> *it was an error: wherefore should God be angry at*
> *thy voice, and destroy the work of thine hands?*

Several things are clear from the scripture. First, any vow carries a great penalty when broken which is why we are warned that it is better not to make them at all, then to make them and break them. We are called foolish when we bind ourselves before God and his messengers (both human and angelic) and then fail to make good on our oath.

Second, the text makes it clear that a broken, solemn vow rises to such a degree of offense in God's sight, that the breach triggers the kind of divine judgement which will affect our home, our family, and our dreams... the writer of Ecclesiastes calls it *"the work of thine hands."* This judgement then certainly can be viewed as a generational curse.

Third and finally, the underlined text referenced above, *"wherefore should God be angry at thy voice,"* would indicate that a broken vow carries the additional harm of making our very prayers void and noneffectual. In consideration of all of this, is it not especially disastrous to break marriage vows which are witnessed by man, angels, and priests; and ratified by God?

Divorce Affects our Inheritance in the Kingdom of God

There is yet another danger in not repenting of the sin of divorce while we still draw breath. The text gives both a dire warning, and yet provides a bright ray of hope for the guilty. It is found in 1 Corinthians 6: 9,10

> *Know ye not that the unrighteous shall not inherit*
> *the kingdom of God? Be not deceived: neither*

> *fornicators*, nor idolaters, nor <u>adulterers</u>, nor
> effeminate, nor abusers of themselves with
> mankind, nor thieves, nor covetous, nor
> drunkards, no revilers, nor extortioners, shall
> inherit the kingdom of God.

As has been demonstrated in Chapter Three, God's definition of adultery is drastically different from ours. He defines an adulterer as one who was married, obtained a divorce, and married another; or, one who marries a divorced person (Matthew 19:9). You will notice from the underlined text printed above that persons who find themselves in either of these categories are numbered with the drunkards, extortioners, thieves, and the whole filthy lot known as the "unrighteous."

What an awful group to be thrown in with!! Worse still, there is the sobering warning that all members of this club will be barred from any inheritance in the Kingdom of God. If you understand that inheritance has everything to do with relationship, than it is plain to see how serious God takes this whole issue of divorce. In other words, God the Father will judge adulterers, and fornicators by taking their birthrights away. If you consider yourself a born-again believer, and fit God's definition of adultery, and have not repented of the specific sin of divorce, the day is going to come when God is going to judge you and disown you.

> *Marriage is honorable in all, and the bed*
> *undefiled; but whoremongers and adulterers God*
> *will judge. Hebrews 13:4*

But wait, thank God for the work of the cross through which we have redemption in the precious Name of Jesus. There is a way out. In order to have the testimony that God delivers from adultery, the sin of divorce must be repented of, particularly if an ex-spouse is yet living.

You may be wondering right now why repentance at the moment of salvation didn't cover this. Let me explain. If someone was married to another and divorced them (or vice versa), and that someone is now married to someone else, God considers both persons practicing adulterers. God considers both people living in sin. The ONLY way out is to repent for the sins of divorce and adultery, and sever the soul tie with the former spouse(s) in the power of the Name of Jesus.

Can We Talk?

Perhaps this chapter on divorce has been the hardest thus far to stomach. Have you examined what the knot in your stomach means? Why does the very mention of divorce as sin stir such powerful feelings of guilt or conviction in you?

One of the things that I love about God, and admittedly, I have many, is that there is no sin except blasphemy against the Holy Ghost that he will not forgive.

> *Wherefore I say unto you, All manner of sin and blasphemy shall be forgiven unto men: but the blasphemy against the Holy Ghost shall not be forgiven unto men. Matt. 12:31*

Hallelujah! That means if I have committed the sin of divorce, whether God-sanctioned or not, the antidote to my problem is as simple as repentance. That's not hard to do... because everyday I must repent for evil thinking, sins of omission, sins of commission, the sin of worry, the sin of procrastination, the sin of doubt, you name it, I'm accustomed to repenting for sin in order to keep my fellowship clear with God. So, repenting for that terrible mistake I made of marrying outside the will of God is easy to do.

What becomes a problem, and it tends to be a problem in all cases of unrepentant sin, is that we don't want to confess our part in the mess we get ourselves into. In other words, it is a trap of the human condition to not want to be held accountable. We would rather stand justified in our own sight, and smugly insinuate that God somehow had some role to play in our messes because he didn't stop us or warn us.

> *Wilt thou also disannul my judgment? wilt thou condemn me, that thou mayest be righteous? Hast*

thou an arm like God? or canst thou thunder with a voice like him? Job 40:8,9

Repenting is one part of the solution; asking God's pardon for the broken covenant is the other part of it. He is the one who must ultimately disannul your broken marital vows, because he is the one who ratified that vow. No, he may not have been pleased with your choice to begin with, but because he honors marriage, he honored your choice. Yes, you adhered to the laws of the land in dissolving your marriage, but you forgot to adhere to the most sacred of all laws — your neglected to pay your vows. A time of reckoning must come — sooner or later, it must come. One way or the other, you must deal with the one who heard your vows, honored them, and who is now incensed that you have broken those vows and ignored him as if his opinion didn't matter. It is a supreme act of rebellion.

As long as you are living, you have a chance to get things right for yourself, your current spouse, and for your descendants. Why not do it right now?

Applying What You Have Learned

1. Why is it so necessary to view divorce as sin? Why isn't it sufficient just to see it as a mistake that had to be fixed?

2. Why does the Apostle Paul appear to raise a harsher standard for the conditions of remarriage than Jesus? How do you reconcile the differences (if there are any) in each of their beliefs regarding an individual's spiritual license to remarry?

3. What kind of curse does divorce set in motion?

4. In 1 Corinthians 6:9,10 when the Word says adulterers and fornicators would not "inherit" the kingdom of God, was he talking about the great by-in-by? If, in fact, he was talking about our entering into his rest right here in this earthly realm, is it possible that an unrepentant act of divorce is affecting your (or your descendants) spiritual condition right now? How so?

5. Perhaps this chapter on divorce does not directly affect you. What did you gain from it anyhow?

Chapter Five

The Soul Tie of Fornication

Seeing Fornication as a Violation of Spiritual Laws

The soul tie which results from fornication is an unholy one, and perhaps the most well known. There are several key problems which the sin of fornication produces in a life. The most quoted scripture on the topic, 1 Corinthians 6:16-18, says that it is the one peculiar sin that a person commits against their own body.

> *What? Know ye not that he which is joined to a harlot is one body? For two saith he, shall be one flesh. But he that is joined unto the Lord is one spirit. Flee fornication. Every sin that a man doeth is without the body; but he that committeth fornication sinneth against his own body.*

A close look at how a soul tie is formed should help explain the peculiarity of the sin committed. The strength of a soul tie is in the joining. Although one does not have to be sexually intimate with someone or something for *joining* to occur, the soul tie which results from vows, oaths, and covenants do involve an intimate embrace of philosophy and mindset. The sexual joining which occurs in fornication is spiritually more powerful, in that it involves two persons becoming one flesh in God's sight.

Herein lies the danger of the soul tie of fornication. The sexual joining binds one soul to another outside the protection and shield of the marriage covenant. This is why we speak of sexual intimacy as a *consummation* of the marriage covenant vows. (Notice that we never speak of fornication as consummating anything!) The vows that one takes in the marital covenant are sacred and binding; but the sexual intimacy that follows is what actually glues the two together in the flesh and results in a unique blood covenant between the two.

There is also the fact that fornication is a violation of a spiritual law, which God has promised will carry a penalty of specific judgment (Galatians 5:19-21; Ephesians 5:3).

> *Marriage is honorable in all, and the bed undefiled: but <u>whoremongers</u> and adulterers God will judge. Hebrews 13:4*

Since God has ordained marriage, and ordained that sexual intimacy consummate the marriage covenant, any violation of that ordinance results in an *illegal joining*. It follows then that if fornication is sin, and it results in illegal joining, then demonic influences are able to gain legal entry. This breach provides an opening, or what can be called "legal ground" for any number of female (or male) ailments. These then result in generational curses, plagues (or what we call sexually transmitted diseases), and shame. In addition, it opens the door for a host of other sexual sins like promiscuity, perverseness, pornography, bestiality, masturbation, unclean thoughts and habits, peeping, homosexuality, transvestitism, licentiousness, riotous living, and all types of seductions.

What of an individual who lives the kind of lifestyle where they become sexually joined to any number of different people in the course of their life? First, such an individual has made a blood covenant (through sexual intimacy) with every person s/he has joined with. Therefore, there is the transgression of a covenant involved.

Second, in that the individual is joined to as many people as s/he was sexually intimate with, very powerful sexual demons have gained a significant foothold in that life which will have an impact on a future, healthy marriage. Unless the soul tie of fornication is broken with all former lovers, the soul ties are retained and that individual remains joined to all of them through the requirements of the collective blood covenants undertaken with them.

Apparently, the peculiar spiritual crime that results from fornication is such a felony, that the Apostle Paul forbade the brethren to even sit down to dine with a known fornicator!

> *But now I have written unto you not to keep company, if any man that is called a brother be a fornicator, or covetous, or an idolator, or a railer, or a drunkard, or an extortioner; with such an one no not to eat. 1 Corinthians 5:11*

Can you now understand why the illegal joining that occurs through fornication results in sin against one's own body? God sanctions sexual intimacy in marriage and makes the male and female one flesh, or one body. He joins their bodies into one flesh. The marriage covenant, when it is honored by both partners, then acts as a shield against sexually transmitted diseases and plagues, and will protect children who are products of that union.

Disaster in the Spirit Realm

Illegal joining, that is, sexual intimacy without covering, means one individual can become one flesh with any number of persons. One shudders to think of what this multiple "oneness" produces in the spirit realm. But, I strongly believe that the Holy Spirit has honored me with a glimpse. Let me share it with you. One day, while preparing this book, the Holy Spirit directed me to look at the sin of Sodom/Gomorrah, indicating to me that the episode held the missing insight that I had been searching for. A word used in the text not only grabbed my attention immediately, but led me into a deeper understanding of the disaster that sexual sin causes in the spirit realm.

In this quite extraordinary story, we get a prelude to the catastrophe that is about to happen to Sodom/Gomorrah in a dialog that includes Abraham and two heavenly visitors. Here's a portion of the text from Genesis 18:20, 21:

> *And the Lord said, Because the <u>cry</u> of Sodom and Gomorrah is great, and because their sin is very grievous; I will go down now, and see whether they have done altogether according to the <u>cry</u> of it, which is come unto me; and if not, I will know.*

That same word "cry" is used again in Genesis 19:13 when the destroying angels lead Lot, his wife and his two daughters out of the doomed city of Sodom. That word for "cry" in Hebrew is *zaaq* and it means to *shriek*. The King James translation of "cry" weakens the strength of the term. This shriek could not have been a band of prayer intercessors crying out to God for the sins of the doomed cities, because the text makes it clear that there were not even ten righteous people in these cities. Even Lot's spiritual condition was suspect — so we are left to wonder if there was even one righteous person in any of the cities!

Who? — or What? was doing the shrieking??? As I delved deeper into the details of this shameful account, I discovered that just about every sexual sin that currently troubles America was prevalent in the cities involved. Chapter 19 of the text describes how Lot persuaded the two angels who appeared as young men to take accommodations for the night in the security of his home. During the course of the evening, the men of the city the Bible says young and old — came to Lot's house and demanded that the two young men come out so that they could have sex with them. Lot does an unspeakable thing to protect the angels — he offers up his virgin daughters with the bargain to the men of the city that they could do with his daughters whatever they pleased — only agree to leave the young men alone! Considering the violent and sexual intent of the crowd of men, is there any wonder what they would have done to his daughters?!

Both daughters were engaged to be married; and it is evident from the text that their intended spouses were part of the group which demanded sexual favors of the angels. The text is clear that all of the men of the city, as well as probably some women, were part of the marauding group. Later, when Lot and his daughters take refuge in Zoar from the fiery destruction of the cities of the plain, his daughters trick him into having sex with them. Within the recounting of two chapters of narrative, we gain a birds-eye view of the prevalence of sexual sin in these cities. We see the actual and latent sins of promiscuity, homosexuality, bisexuality, incest, fornication, prostitution, and rape. The Bible says that their sin shrieked to the very heights of the Mountain of God.

> *And the Lord said, Because the cry of Sodom and Gomorrah is great, and because their sin is very grievous; I will go down now, and see whether they have <u>done altogether according to the cry of it, which is come unto me</u>; and if not, I will know.*
> *Genesis 18: 20, 21*

Could it be that sin creates such a tumult in the spirit realm — that it unsettles a spiritual equilibrium? Could it be that sin has a voice, and that some sins are louder than others? The Bible records two examples of sin that are so egregious that they actually have voices that "shriek" — thereby disturbing something in the spirit realm. The first recorded example is in Genesis 4:10 and then again in Revelations 6:10 where blood spilled as a result of murder cries out (shrieks) from the ground. The final example is in

our text Genesis 18:20; 19:13 where the sexual sins of
Sodom and Gomorrah shrieked — so much so that the Lord
told Abraham that the sins were "grievous." If, in fact, sexual sin in particular causes an unusual disturbance in the
spirit realm, we get a glimpse of the shrieking that must go
on when people engage in wanton harlotry.

Breaking Multiple-Lover Soul Ties

Any form of sexual intimacy, outside of marriage, is considered fornication. When one considers that any prelude to
sex in the form of petting and fondling is little more than
foreplay, then one can hardly argue that sexual activity has
not occurred. Further, when we yield any part of our members willingly to a member of the opposite sex for the purpose of intimacy or to fulfill a lustful attraction, we have
committed the sin of fornication. The Apostle Paul had this
to say in Romans 6:16 and 19:

> *Know ye not, that to whom ye yield yourselves*
> *servants to obey, his servants ye are to whom ye*
> *obey; whether of sin unto death, or of obedience unto*
> *righteousness? I speak after the manner of men*
> *because of the infirmity of your flesh: for as ye have*
> *yielded your members servants to uncleanness and*
> *to iniquity unto iniquity; even so now yield your*
> *members servants to righteousness unto holiness.*

Soul ties with multiple lovers are broken in the same
way that any other soul tie is broken. Although these lovers
are part of a past life, an individual is still joined to them in
the flesh because of the blood covenant which results from
sexual intimacy. Of a certainty, during the illegal sexual act,
there was a transference of unclean spirits that occurred.
When the sin of fornication is committed, a demonic spirit
joins the two together in an unholy blood covenant.

Further, when that spirit joins the two fornicators, that spirit makes sure that the man gets whatever is bothering her, and she gets whatever is bothering him. Believers have the authority to cast these spirits out of themselves in the Name of Jesus; but unless the soul tie is broken, demons have every right to return whenever they like — after all, it was the demon that formed the unholy soul tie in the first place. It becomes their habitation. Perhaps this will solve the mystery of why some people can break free from some sins for a while, and then they find themselves drawn back into bondage to the same thing. To repeat, these demons have a legal right to harass that individual who has not severed unholy soul ties — demons have carte blanche to return to their "houses" if the soul tie is retained.

To dethrone them forever, there must be repentance made regarding the peculiar sin of fornication which was committed against their own body. All soul ties with all lovers should be renounced name by name. Then, repentance must be made for breaking the law of God regarding the sanctuary of the Holy Spirit (1 Thessalonians 4:3; 1 Corinthians 6:19), which is our body. All demons associated with the illegal joining(s) should be commanded to leave and the body should be declared to now be the clean, undefiled temple of the Holy Ghost. Finally, all doorways should be sealed which are opened to the enemy through ignorance.

The Need for More Cleansing

Cleansing is now only partly complete. To be free completely, you must rid yourself of all jewelry, photos, keepsakes, mementos, etc. given to you by your former lovers or which represent old lovers. All of them must be destroyed with the same vehemence as you would any familiar object. Finally, to remain free, make a decision once and for all about separating from all old lovers. Remember that the strength of a soul tie is in the joining. That joining is not just physical, but it is spiritual.

It is important that you serve notice to your former lovers that the relationship is over, including intermittent phone calls, the walks and intimate talks in the park, and the sweet no-harm greeting cards loaded with innuendo. That means being honest with yourself about any contrived justification for remaining "friends" with someone who used to be a former lover.

Perhaps you married your lover and are wondering about the fornication soul tie that was formed before the covenant of marriage was sealed by God. You cannot make an unholy thing holy. The demon who first joined the two of you by way of illegal sexual intimacy has staked out a claim in your marriage because quite frankly, that demon joined the two of you before God did! You must repent, renounce and banish all demons associated with the fornication soul tie from your marriage. This is a good example of where the past can come back to haunt you.

Illegitimate Children: Forgotten Victims

Let's turn our attention for a moment to children which are conceived as a result of fornication. Children tend to be the overlooked casualty in ungodly relationships. So sacred is the covering of marriage that even if a spouse is a non-believer, God will consider the child(ren) holy based on a believing spouse's relationship with him.

> *For the unbelieving husband is sanctified by the wife, and the unbelieving wife is sanctified by the husband: else were your children unclean; but now are they holy. 1 Corinthians 7:14*

That word for sanctify in the Greek is *hagiazo*. It means to make holy, to hallow, or to purify or consecrate. What the

Apostle was setting forth here is the whole principle of "covering." Just one believer in a marriage is good enough to sanctify the marriage itself and any children produced from it. This covering carries great weight of authority in the spirit realm.

It bears noting, however, that children who are not so covered by the marriage covenant, will be impacted by a little-known generational curse which has its origins in the Old Testament. It is found in Deuteronomy 23:2:

> *A bastard shall not enter into the congregation of the Lord; even to his tenth generation shall he not enter into the congregation of the Lord.*

The transference of spirits, which occurs in illegal joining, also forms a portal into the soul of your unborn children because they are spiritually "uncovered" or unclean. In addition, children born "uncovered" will be open prey for sexual plagues as well as any number of generational curses set in motion as a result of the peculiar sin of fornication.

To cleanse and dedicate your children who were born through illegal joining, you must repent, renounce, and sever your soul tie with the natural parent of your child. Your goal in doing so is not to separate your child from his/her parent, but to sever the unholy soul tie between you and the child's other parent. You must not forget to command all demons which entered your child's life to depart and to take their goods with them. Declare your child free from demonic interference and cleansed by the blood of Jesus Christ. Remember that your child is protected by the walk you have in Christ. Understanding the authority you have in Christ will go a long way in setting your child free of the sins of your past.

If you so desire, and feel led to do so, have your pastor or one in spiritual authority over you lay hands on your child and say a prayer of consecration over their lives and bless them. If you are now married to a believer who is not the natural parent of your child, that step-parent may exert his spiritual authority over the child (particularly a step-father) and also declare your child blessed and covered.

Can We Talk?

No matter what kind of sexual sin we are talking about, inevitably, it had its roots in the first sin of fornication. That is one of the reasons that God takes such a hard line against it. Once you get started in sexual sin, the door is opened for progressively worse acts of sexual degradation and deviation. But if you and I are being honest about the matter, usually a stronghold of sexual indiscretion starts out as a single act of casual sex. From there, you become a person so hungry for physical contact and intimacy, that you lose your own sense of boundaries and personal conviction regarding the sacredness of sex. It is a dangerous thing that has historically plagued the Body of Christ since the very start of the New Testament Church.

Let's talk for a moment about what you have learned in this chapter. By now, you should have a clear understanding that you are joined to every single person that you have ever had casual sex with, regardless of whether you were married to them. (Unless, of course, you knew enough about soul ties before this book to have severed those joinings in the Name of Jesus.) By now, you should understand that the task of severing those unholy ties begins with repentance and a prayer command to the demons involved that those ties are forever broken. That's the simple part.

The more difficult part is the cleansing that follows. This is what will require faith and conviction. The first part, the Holy Spirit does for you as you take that stand in the Name of Jesus. The second part will require some work on your part: and that is getting rid of the mementoes, the old love letters, and the photos you have tucked away but which are definitely not in the photo albums you have displayed in your living room for public viewing.

How much does total victory mean to you? Does that stack of faded love letters hold more value than the health of your soul? The crazy part about it is that the love affair with your old flame wasn't even all that great. That's why you are not with that individual today. So why are reveling in the memory of what presents itself as a former great love, when the reality is that while you were involved with that person the relationship was one-dimensional, sometimes crazy, maybe violent, sometimes manipulative, and always dysfunctional? Get real!

What you need to do is to pull down that stronghold in your imagination. And, if you would be honest with yourself, the fact is, whenever you see that person now that you're saved, you have had numerous occasions to wonder what in the Name of God you ever saw in that person to begin with. But what you are doing is looking with regenerated eyes. So since your eyes are regenerated, regenerate your memory — that old relationship was not all that great! Get rid of the stuff that belonged to your former lover. Now that the skunk is gone (no pun intended), you should want its odor gone too.

One final consideration: sex is the act of marriage. When God created sex, he created it to be sweet, fun, satisfying, and spiritual. So special was it in the sight and purpose of God, that he put a fence around it. That fence is marked, "For married, grown folks only."

Applying What You Have Learned

1. Identify three things you have learned about fornication soul ties thus far in the book.

2. Explain why you believe it is necessary to break friendship and communication with old lovers.

3. Based on your knowledge that soul ties are not just formed through intimacy, but can be formed in other ways, is it possible that your children formed soul ties with your ex-flames? Considering the emotional rollercoaster you went through in breaking off with them, what do you think your children went through when you broke off with them?

4. If your children were the product of fornication — which left them spiritually uncovered, what can you do now to create a covering for them?

5. In 1 Corinthians 6:18, the Apostle Paul states that every sin is without the body, but he that commits fornication, sins against their own body. What is it about sexual sin that causes this peculiar violation against one's own flesh?

6. The scripture talks specifically of two kinds of sin, fornication being one of them, that has a voice. What is the other one?

7. What is the Greek word for fornication in scripture, and what acts of sexual sin does it include?

65

Chapter Six

Soul Ties with Demons

How they Gain Legal Ground

Demons must cross legal boundaries set by God to have leave to torment or oppress believers. Spiritually speaking, we give demons "legal ground" or "legal rights" by touching, handling, and tasting unclean things which God has forbidden.

> *Be ye not unequally yoked together with unbelievers; for what fellowship hath righteousness with unrighteousness? And what communion hath light with darkness? And what concord hath Christ with Belial? Or what part hath he that believeth with an infidel? And what agreement hath the temple of God with idols? For ye are the temple of the living God; as God hath said, I will dwell in them, and walk in them; and I will be their God, and they shall be my people.*
> *2 Corinthians 6:14-16*

As we have been teaching throughout, the strength of a soul tie is in the joining. In marriage, that joining takes the form of covenant vows and sexual intimacy. In fornication, that joining takes the form of illegal sexual intimacy. With secular organizations, joining occurs through spoken vows, oaths, covenants and agreements. In the case of demons, joining occurs through fellowship. For example, an individual is able to achieve fellowship or joining with demons through occultic contact. This includes sorcery (hallucinogenic and illicit drugs), astrology, witchcraft, palm reading, consulting with mediums, etc.

In addition, what the Bible terms "familiar objects" are unclean objects which have been anointed by demons and are in the possession of a human being. These include (to name but a few) fetishes, cultural tribal masks (any tribal mask with an object piercing its nose will summon the spirit of death), and some cultural artifacts. Demons consider those objects as giving them legal ground to inhabit a building or house. In addition, they create all kinds of demonic havoc in your home-including disharmony in your marriage. Look at this strong prohibition against the possession of such objects from Deuteronomy 7:26:

> *Neither shalt thou bring an abomination into thine house, lest thou be a cursed thing like it: but thou shall utterly detest it, and thou shalt utterly abhor it: for it is a cursed thing.*

Other things that lead to fellowship with demons include tatooing, hypnotism, mind control games, blood covenants and rituals, body-piercing, anything that results in mutilation or ritualistic cutting of the body, and anything that requires the implant of a needle such as in acupuncture should be considered a violation of God's commandments regarding our bodies. Of a certainty, these things will lead to soul ties with demons.

As contemporary believers we don't often stop and think about the seriousness of idolatry. In an Old Testament context, it is easy to define what an idol is and why God abhorred them so much. Today, we have idols which are just as abominable — they just don't have false heads and arms the way Baal worshipers once fashioned their gods. We need to stop and consider that many of us have abominable objects and artifacts in our homes which God finds obnoxious. Our refusal to part with such objects, particularly if our allegiance to them is based on their value, sends a clear signal to the demons attached thereto that we are in agreement with them. The prophet Amos begs the question,

Can two walk together, except they be agreed?
Amos 3:3

There are also those who believe that you can sanctify an unholy thing. That is, there are some that suggest that the way to keep an unclean object that may be of sentimental value to you is to sanctify it. How can that be? If a thing is altogether unclean and demonic in its conception, that is, it was produced for the purpose of iniquity or unrighteousness, by what means can it be consecrated? Things that are carnal can be consecrated unto a holy use, but I dare say that one can consecrate an abominable thing unto a holy use.

One final way that a demonic soul tie is formed is when an individual rejects the Word or is offended because of it, and chooses to return to an unclean lifestyle or habit. Indulgence is considered the practice of sin, and will open an individual to very serious demonic oppression.

> *When the unclean spirit is gone out of a man, he walketh through dry places, seeking rest, and findeth none. Then he saith, I will return into my house from whence I came out; and when he is come, he findeth it empty, swept, and garnished. Then goeth he, and taketh with himself seven other spirits more wicked than himself, and they enter in and dwell there: and the last state of that man is worse than the first. Even so shall it be also unto this wicked generation. Matthew 12:43-45*

Severing the Soul tie with a Demon

To sever the soul tie with a demon, you must repent, renounce involvement in activity which is occultic, and command all demons that entered your life to go at once. Further cleansing may be needed even after you destroy occultic artifacts and objects. You will probably need to hallow the ground and atmosphere where the objects were situated through a prayer of cleansing. Your authority over these demons must be firm and specific. If it is imprudent to burn occultic objects, remove them from your possession at once and do not make them available to another unsuspecting person. On that note, be wary of purchasing jewelry and artifacts from second-hand stores and garage sales unless you know something about the habits and lifestyle of the previous owner.

If you have engaged in acupuncture, body piercing, body mutilation, tattooing, or the like, more than likely you are at present under constant and fierce torment by demons. You should enlist the aid of a pastor or someone who walks in deliverance ministry. They will be completely unable to help you unless you are serious about doing everything necessary to get free and stay free from the demonic soul ties which have been formed.

Applying What You Have Learned

1. Name five ways that people inadvertently invite fellowship with demons.

2. When an object is altogether unholy in its origin, nature, and purpose, can you sanctify it using the authority you have in the Name of Jesus?

3. What does it mean that a demon has to have "legal ground" to torment an human being? If Christians belong to Jesus, how can it be that they have any legal basis to torment us?

4. What is a familiar object? Give a few examples. What kind of "anointing" have demons placed on these objects?

5. How do you sever the soul tie with a demon?

6. Besides the possession of objects, there are certain things that people do to their bodies which lead to demonic oppression. Name 4.

Chapter Seven

Restoration of the Soul

Repentance is the First Step

> For what shall it profit a man, if he shall gain the whole world, and lose his own soul? Or what shall a man give in exchange for his soul? Mark 8:36,37

After reading this book, perhaps many of you are feeling that the dire warnings contained herein have not affected your life one bit. Perhaps you believe, as a divorced and remarried person, that if in fact soul ties were so dangerous, the blessings of the Lord would not be so prevalent in your life. Think again.

> ...For he maketh his sun to rise on the evil and on the good, and sendeth rain on the just and on the unjust. Matthew 5:45b

God is good to all, and his benefits extend to every soul under the heavens. His mercy and his grace are without end. None of us can ever afford to think that because we have gotten by, it means we have gotten away. There are always consequences for violating God's Word. Unfortunately, when we refuse to do what is necessary to pay our debts and oaths, sometimes the penalty for breaking covenant with God must be paid by our children and our children's children. Our way out is always a simple one: repentance. God wants godly sorrow, from our hearts, when we have broken his commandments. It is not always convenient to take steps to right our wrongs. Thank God for repentance which gives us a second chance — especially when we can't undo what we have done wrong.

There is no restoration of the soul without repentance. Only redemption provides the basis for wholeness and holiness. Jesus is the only truth, the only light, and the only way. Throughout eternity, God the Father has determined that unless we come through the Son, we cannot have life. As you repent to the Son, the soul — which is lawless, and impudent — even arrogant, must submit its willfulness to the regenerated self, which is the spirit of a man. To refuse to repent, is to allow the soul man to have the last say in your future.

The scriptures are clear about God's feelings toward sexual sin, especially adultery and divorce. To treat these scriptures with contempt is a mistake. To dismiss them as no longer relevant for today or for your situation is the luxury of foolish men who don't know Jesus as Lord. There is a much-quoted scripture that is little understood; I wonder if it may shed some light on those who will one day stand before Father God and find that they have been disowned. It is found in Matthew 7:21-27.

> *Not every one that saith unto me, Lord, Lord, shall enter into the kingdom of heaven; but he that doeth the will of my Father which is in heaven. Many will say to me in that day, Lord, Lord, have we not prophesied in thy name? and in thy name have cast out devils? and in thy name done many wonderful works? And then will I profess unto them, I never knew you: depart from me, ye that work iniquity. Therefore whosoever heareth these sayings of mine, and doeth them, I will liken him unto a wise man, which built his house upon a rock: And the rain descended, and the floods came, and the winds blew, and beat upon that house; and it fell not: for it was founded upon a rock. And every one that heareth these sayings of mine, and doeth them not, shall be likened unto a*

foolish man, which built his house upon the sand: And the rain descended, and the floods came, and the winds blew, and beat upon that house; and it fell: and great was the fall of it.

I believe, as you do, that once I repent as a sinner and make Jesus Savior and Lord of my life, that I move from the "sinner, saved by grace" category, into the category of the righteous. No, I don't believe that it is then necessary to live out my life afraid of some sin that I forgot to repent for. Like you, I believe that once I am redeemed by the Blood of the Lamb, that my life is forever hid in Him. However, if I am living in sin, that makes me a practitioner of sin. That means that calling Jesus "Lord, Lord" in church and in my home or wherever, will profit me nothing in the day that I stand before him to give account of what I have said and done in this flesh. Worse, is the prospect that after all of my preaching and teaching, and all the demons I wore out, in the Last Day, I myself should be found to be a castaway.

But I keep under my body, and bring it into subjection: lest that by any means, when I have preached to others, I myself should be a castaway. 1 Corinthians 9:27

In that day, God forbid that you or I should be denied by the Son before the Father. Such a horrible fate can be prevented through the plan of salvation, which gives us an antidote for every sin. That antidote is called repentance.

A Prayer to Break Soul Ties

Once you have repented, break the unholy soul tie — whatever it may be. You do that in the Name of Jesus. Here is a prayer to pray if you are breaking a soul tie that was formed through fornication (sexual sin).

Father God, in the Name of your Son Jesus, I come to your throne of grace repenting for the sin of fornication which I have committed in violation of your laws. I ask that you would forgive me and pardon me for every transgression associated with this act. As you pardon me, dear Lord, I pray that you would also cleanse me and make me whole. In your Name, Jesus, I cancel every curse that I have set in motion in the spirit realm as a result of my sin. Your Word says, that "the curse causeless shall not stand." I stand on the power of that word right now, and cast down every plan that the enemy had designed for my life. I thank you and receive your pardon for my sin, and I praise you Lord Jesus that I have absolution and redemption because of your Blood and the work you accomplished for me on the Cross.

Father God, in the Name of your Son Jesus, I rebuke every foul, unclean, demonic spirit that has set up a habitation in my body and soul because of this sin. I sever the soul tie with Billy in the Name of Jesus. I forever demolish it and break its power in my soul and in my life. Every demonic spirit that entered my life as a result of this ungodly soul tie, I command to depart right now. I command that these unclean spirits leave me forever, and I destroy their works and their goods in my life. I declare myself to be a vessel of the Holy Spirit; holy, pure, undefiled and sanctified before the Lord my God. I claim the safety and protection of the Blood of Jesus Christ over my life, and the lives of all of my children and descendants. Thank you Lord Jesus, that your Blood washes the very residue, stain, and odor of this sin away from my life, and my children's lives forever. Amen.

The words of this prayer can be changed to accommodate the breaking of any soul tie that the Holy Spirit has revealed as being unholy in your life. It is important where soul ties of sexual sin or divorce is concerned, that you name the individuals involved. Do the same thing regarding the ungodly vows you took with organizations and secret fraternities. Name the organization, and specify the words of the vow or oath you took. In order to annul the vow, you must be very specific about what it is that you are canceling in the spirit realm.

For instance, if you took a vow to commit your life, body and soul to the tenets and degrees of the First Order of Daffy Duck Templars of the Night, when you break that soul tie, declare the commission of your life, body and soul to the tenets and degrees of the First Order of Daffy Duck Templars of the Night to be set aside, and hereby voided in the Name of Jesus. Remember that if you want the breaking of a soul tie to be effective, you should begin by repenting for the sin. Then, break the soul tie and dismiss all demons associated with the tie. Do all of this in the Name of the Lord Jesus.

In breaking soul ties over your children, you can pray the same model prayer, just remember to reword it to cover your children — and call them by name. Declare your authority over them as parents and guardians — this serves notice to the demons which engineer unholy soul ties that you know who you are and you know what your authority is in Christ Jesus. Then to close your prayer over your children, declare your children to be covered and sealed by the Blood of Jesus Christ.

As a final measure, ask God to close any doorways that demons may have opened in your children's lives. Often, demons will try to leave an opening by which they can gain reentry at some point in the child's life when that child is of legal age to make decisions on their own. Close these doorways in the Name of Jesus.

Final Steps to Restore Your Soul

As we have said throughout, you must forgive the one who has committed sin against your person — whether you were a victim of an unclean act perpetrated against you, or you willingly engaged in the act. Forgiveness does not mean that you consider the harm committed against you as being okay. Forgiveness means that your pardon will free your soul to the point that you can have another chance at life without the pain of the past. If you refuse to forgive, you are forever doomed to live the balance of your days shackled to the one who harmed you. Refusing to forgive, means that you have made a decision to define who you are and what you will ever become by what has happened to you in the past. What a shame — and what a tremendous price to pay for something that you didn't deserve. Jesus, the lover of your soul, wants to give you a bright new hope and usher you into a wonderful new season of life.

> *For I know the thoughts that I think toward you,*
> *saith the LORD, thoughts of peace, and not of evil,*
> *to give you an expected end. Jeremiah 29:11*

Perhaps the matter of forgiveness is not an easy one for you, given the circumstances whereby the unholy soul tie was formed. Perhaps there are so many issues involved, that you don't know where to start with the forgiving that needs to be done. Ask the Holy Spirit to lead you. Allow him to be the master surgeon that he is. He is firm, but very gentle. The hand of the potter is sure and steady... he will not harm you, neither will he move faster with you than you are ready. Trust him at all times.

Finally, in order to see that your soul is restored from the fragmentation of old traumas and hurts, you must pray for yourself. To do this, I recommend praying for yourself everyday in your heavenly language. Look at what the

Apostle Paul had to say about the medicinal effects of praying in tongues.

> *For he that speaketh in an unknown tongue speaketh not unto men, but unto God: for no man understandeth him; howbeit in the spirit he speaketh mysteries. He that speaketh in an unknown tongue edifieth himself; but he that prophesieth <u>edifieth</u> the church. 1 Corinthians 14:2,4*

That underlined word "edify" is oikodomeo in the Greek. Its meaning is, "to be a housebuilder, to build up, or to edify." More importantly, it indicates that praying in the spirit builds up the spirit man. Which is the best way to compel the soul to submit to the work of Christ in your life. I would suggest that as you begin to break soul ties, and dismiss demons associated with these ties from your life, and as you forgive and release, that you do the final important thing, and that is to pray for yourself daily in your tongue language. Make it a habit. Follow up with praise and thanksgiving. And remember that the scripture says,

> *In every thing give thanks: for this is the will of God in Christ Jesus concerning you. 1 Thessalonians 5:18*

Can We Talk?

Now that you have the knowledge, and now that you know what to pray to break unholy soul ties, you are probably needing to know what you can do to move from the place of brokenness to healing. There are many things you can do and several steps you must take.

Earlier in the book, we talked about getting rid of old love-notes, mementoes, jewelry given to you by the former lover, and what have you as an important step in cleansing your personal space. It is important to do this cleansing for your heart too. As long as you keep intimate objects given to you by ex-lovers, your soul will secretly reside in that place of dead things and broken vows. You must make it clear to your soul and your heart, that you will no longer cling to the broken affairs and promises of a life that shall never be. Ridding yourself of these objects has a tremendous impact on the natural realm as well as the spirit realm.

Then, forgiveness, is an important step. You must remember that when your heart has been broken, forgiveness is not something you speak with your mouth, it is a decision you make from your heart. There can be no conditions attached to it whatever, and you must not fool yourself into thinking that because you no longer *feel* hurt that it means you are no longer hurting. The images associated with any past wound is evidence of the stage you are in as far as forgiving. If, like ghostly shadows, certain moments from the past cling around the edges of your memory, there is an issue that is still unsettled. You must settle it once and for all, if you are to walk free of that memory. Face it, confront it, address it, and pursue it for the sake of your life. Decide that unless you take away its ability to torment you, everything is at stake.

Once you conquer something, you must talk and act like a champion. Just because something returns to taunt you, doesn't mean you didn't gain the victory over it. If you know that God has set you free from a thing, why would you allow yourself to be persuaded that you are really not free? When the thing left your life, you were keenly aware of the change. What changed your mind about its exit?

When you gain victory of an enemy that has vanquished your life and left you degraded and impoverished, get indignant enough toward it, that its very smell makes you angry. The Word of God says, *"Submit yourselves therefore to God. Resist the devil, and he will flee from you."* James 4:7 Understand, beloved, that resistance is aggressive, not passive. It does not stand around waiting to get hit, it throws a punch at the first sight of confrontation. That's resistance!

Finally, every time you are faced with a memory of the old soul tie or a reminder of it, do the same thing that you do when the adversary tries to remind you of what you used to be before you came to Christ. Know what your Word says about your freedom. Talk to your soul and to the enemy of your soul in the context of what faith in God's Word has delivered unto you. You have peace through the cross and victory through the shed blood of the Savior. You should not have to be convinced of something that is a fact.

Applying What You Have Learned

1. What is the first step in breaking an unholy soul tie?

2. What effects do unbroken soul ties have on an individual's life?

3. What are God's feelings about sexual sin? Can you give two Biblical examples where wanton sexual sin made God so angry that he destroyed the people involved?

4. If you were to explain to someone who was new to the issue of soul ties how to pray a prayer which would effectively sever unholy soul ties, what specific things would you tell them to include in the prayer?

5. Can this prayer be done by you? Or, to have impact, must it be done by a minister? In whose name will you make sure the prayer is conducted?

6. Why is forgiveness such an important element of breaking soul ties forever? How does unforgiveness hold a soul tie intact?

7. Once the unholy soul tie is broken, how does one get healing for the fragmentation of the soul that resulted while the soul tie was intact?

Chapter Eight

Frequently Asked Questions About Soul Ties

1. *I am a victim of rape. The sexual joining that occurred was completely unwilling on my part. Did this joining result in a soul tie?*

   Answer: Yes. Sexual intimacy, willing or unwilling, always results in a soul tie. In breaking this soul tie, command all spirits of bitterness, anger, rejection, and unforgiveness to leave your life forever.

2. *I am a victim of incest that occurred with one of my natural parents. What soul tie needs to be broken?*

   Answer: The soul tie between a parent and a child is a holy one. The soul tie you described is of unholy origin. Unless broken, very powerful demons will continue to harass you. Sever the soul tie which has resulted from the incest and command all demons which accompanied the trauma to leave in the Name of Jesus.

3. *I have multiple past lovers and am unable to remember all of their names. Will a general prayer of release sever all of them?*

   Answer: Yes. However, it is my experience as a deliverance minister, that the name of each lover needs to be called out in turn, and the soul tie declared broken in Jesus' Name. Bear in mind, that a demon engineered the joining of each lover to your soul. A general prayer of release is not nearly powerful enough to convince each of these demons that they must relinquish their habitation. If you cannot remember all of the names, ask the Holy Spirit to bring each lover's spirit before you — and then expel the demon associated with each lover, in turn. You are then better able to identify what spirits may have entered your life as a result of each relationship. A prayer of forgiveness is always in order for each individual also.

4. *My children were conceived out of wedlock by a man whom they have never met. Should I, and do I have the authority, to sever the soul tie between them and their father?*

   Answer: Yes if you are blood-washed and Spirit filled, you should sever the soul tie between them, and yes you do have the authority. Your children were conceived in sin and were therefore uncovered when they were conceived. The illegal sexual intimacy that occurred between you and their father made them vulnerable to numerous demonic spirits.

   In order to free your children, you must first repent that they were conceived in sin, renounce your behavior as contrary to God's commandments, sever the soul ties involved, and command all demons spirits to leave your children's lives that entered during their conception. Your authority comes through relationship to them as the maternal parent, and through the Cross. Severing the soul tie should not prevent your children from respecting and loving their father if he ever decides to reappear in their lives. It is unwise to even share with your children that you have severed the soul tie. They will not understand the meaning of what you have done, and may one day resent you for it.

5. *I have severed the soul tie with a former lover but I am still plagued by dreams and memories of him. Is there anything I have left undone?*

   Answer: Have you forgiven him? Forgiveness is not a feeling, it is an act. It also involves stages which include identifying the specific harm, confronting the anger, releasing the need for retribution, and praying for him. In addition, do you still have jewelry or mementoes from him? Discard them or give them away. Have you commanded all spirits which entered your life through the break up or fornication to leave? You must do so, or the soul tie is retained.

6. *How long does it take to stop feeling the effects of an illegal soul tie?*

    Answer: If you have severed it and commanded all spirits associated with it to leave, then you should feel the effects of the release in 3 months or less. If after 6 months you still feel emotional pain, there is something that you have left undone.

7. *Can I declare soul ties broken over somebody else's life?*

    Answer: It depends on who the somebody else is. If the other person is unrelated to you by immediate family blood ties, you will not be able to effectively break ungodly soul ties in their lives. If they are, you may have some limited authority to break them. Remember, however, that their will is involved. You do have the authority on the request of another believer to pray a prayer to break soul ties, especially if that individual is unsure of how to do it and has given you authority to pray over them for the breakage.

8. *I have broken all known ungodly soul ties in my life. Why am I still oppressed by unclean thoughts?*

    Answer: There was more than one demon involved in each tie. One engineered the tie and then invited his buddies in. Ask the Holy Spirit to reveal the identities of these other spirits, call them by name in turn, and cast them out of yourself in the Name of Jesus. Demand that they take all of their "goods" with them.

9. *What is the harm in remaining "just friends" with former lovers?*

    Answer: It depends on how far you take the "just friends" part. If you are now married, or dating someone else, what purpose does your "just friends" relationship with that former lover serve? You are deceiving yourself. Clearly, your soul tie is retained. If the soul tie is truly severed, you should have absolutely no desire to continue any type of bond with your former lover. If you tend to feel defensive when the question arises, you should take that as an indication that you have not truly severed the soul tie.

10. *What if my husband (or wife) still has soul ties with former lovers or an ex-spouse? Do I have the authority to sever my spouse's ungodly soul ties?*

    Answer: Yes, only to a VERY limited extent. Although you are now the spouse of covenant, there is someone (the ex) who preceded you in that distinction. They too share authority over your spouse. You must repent for you and your spouse for the sin of divorce and adultery, first. Then, you can break the soul ties with the ex and with former lovers of your spouse by exerting your authority as the present (and blood-washed believing) spouse of covenant. On that authority, pray an intercessory prayer to repent, renounce and break all former ties. Then do a prayer of release and cleansing over your spouse. It is even more powerful if you can get your spouse to touch and agree with what you are doing.

11. *How can I stop my ex-husband from hindering my prayers (canceling my vows) in the spirit realm?*

    Answer: First, repent for the sins of adultery and divorce. If you are now remarried and your husband is a believer, have him exert his authority as your covering to nullify any authority that your ex-husband retains. In any event, sever the soul tie with your former husband and repent for the sin of breaking those covenant vows. Although your divorce/separation from your husband may be entirely justifiable, they were covenant vows which were made and broken. Repentance is in order.

12. *How do unbroken soul ties affect my marriage? What are the negative impacts?*

    Answer: Too numerous to list, but here are a few. If you have children, they are affected in many ways. Your marital relations (intimacy) with your spouse may be affected. You may find yourself comparing your spouse to former lovers. You can expect feelings of distrust and even rejection from your spouse. In addition, you will intermittently experience problems with lust and longing — for other people. There may be times when you will have the odd feeling of wanting to change your spouse into someone else — although you will not know exactly who or what. Spiritually speaking, unbroken soul ties will hinder your prayer life, because you are joined in the spirit realm to other people besides just your spouse.

13. *My mother-in-law has an unhealthy sway over my husband. Can this soul tie be broken between them?*

    Answer: Soul ties between parents and children are considered holy and insoluble until death. Hence, parents retain some measure of authority over their children even after they reach adulthood. When, however, we transgress lines of authority regarding the law of *leaving and cleaving* in marriage, it causes chaos in the spirit realm.

    God has provided balance in the parent-to-child authority relationship by giving men the authority of *leaving and cleaving* which makes the marital covenant tenable. Men who fail to exert this authority over their mothers, leave their wives and their marriage vulnerable to attacking spirits of oppression and manipulation. The soul tie between your mother and your husband is not likely to be broken, but the problem can be resolved if your husband is ever able to break free of the spirit of witchcraft with which his mother controls him.

14. *You stated in your book that God considers the marriage covenant insoluble. Why does God consider the covenant of marriage so sacred?*

    Answer: In marriage, the covenant of marriage was cut in Adam's flesh by God himself. In fact, it is called the "Covenant of God" (see Proverbs 2:17 and Malachi 2:14). The Hebrew term for covenant is *berith*. Biblically, we gain a better understanding of covenant in the context of animal sacrifices. When two animals were cut or divided in two, the smoke of the Lord passed between the parts ratifying the covenant (see Genesis 15). Also recall that the physical act of circumcision was a sign cut in a male's flesh signifying the Abrahamic covenant.

15. *Can I break soul ties with my ex-husband, even if he has refused to grant me a divorce?*

    Answer: Because of the uniqueness of the marriage soul tie, the question you raise is troublesome. A man gains great spiritual authority over the wife in the marriage covenant. A man who refuses to release his wife from their marriage vows, even if he is a non-believer, can greatly hinder although not entirely block his former wife's prayers. Although God considers a man's act of putting away his wife as a supreme act of rebellion (Malachi 3:14), if your husband has broken God's commandments with respect to his love for you (Ephesians 5:28), or if he has committed adultery, it may be that this is sufficient grounds to break soul ties with him. If he has committed adultery on you, in God's eyes the marriage vows are canceled already. In such a case, you are free, but you still need to sever the soul tie. By the way, if you are separated and not legally and spiritually divorced, you are barred from dating someone else.

16. *Can one have a soul tie with someone you have not been intimate with?*

    Answer: Yes. Some are holy, some are unholy. In a fellowship of believers, we are told to bear one another's burdens (Galatians 6:2). Godly soul ties allow us to do this within divinely sanctioned boundaries (for example, we don't disrupt the covenant relationship between married persons in the same fellowship of believers). Friendship soul ties between persons of the same gender are clearly unhealthy when the relationship becomes possessive, or when co-dependency develops. Finally, soul ties can also develop when a person lusts or longs for another person (unrequited love), or if someone were to fall in love with someone else.